The Roman Republic: A Very Short Introduction

Titles in the series include the following:

David M. Gwynn

THE ROMAN REPUBLIC

A Very Short Introduction

OXFORD
UNIVERSITY PRESS

OXFORD
UNIVERSITY PRESS

Great Clarendon Street, Oxford, OX2 6DP,
United Kingdom

Oxford University Press is a department of the University of Oxford.
It furthers the University's objective of excellence in research, scholarship,
and education by publishing worldwide. Oxford is a registered trade mark of
Oxford University Press in the UK and in certain other countries

© David M. Gwynn 2012

The moral rights of the author have been asserted

First Edition published in 2012

British Library Cataloguing in Publication Data
Data available

Library of Congress Cataloging in Publication Data
Data available

ISBN 978-0-19-959511-2

Printed and bound by
CPI Group (UK) Ltd, Croydon, CR0 4YY

Contents

List of illustrations

List of maps

The publisher and author apologize for any errors or omissions. If
contacted they will be happy to rectify these at the earliest opportunity.

Introduction

The rise and fall of the Roman Republic occupies a special place in the history of Western civilization. From humble beginnings on seven hills beside the River Tiber, the city of Rome grew to dominate the ancient Mediterranean world. Led by the senatorial aristocracy, Republican armies defeated Carthage and the successor kingdoms to Alexander the Great, and brought the surrounding peoples to east and west under Roman rule. Yet the triumph of the Republic was also its tragedy. The very forces that drove the expansion of Rome, and the rewards that expansion brought, led to social, economic, and political crisis and plunged the Republic into a descending spiral of civil war. The institutions of Republican government failed under the pressures of maintaining Rome's empire, and sole power finally passed into the hands of Augustus, the first Roman emperor.

For subsequent generations, the Roman Republic has offered a model, a source of inspiration, and a cautionary tale. The myths of the Roman past, its literature and art, and the heroes and villains of the Republic have never ceased to stir the imagination. Novels, films, and television series continue to exploit that legacy to this day, with widely varying degrees of historical accuracy. Yet the Republic's history is as gripping as any fiction. It includes moments of highest drama, from the Gallic Sack of Rome and Hannibal crossing the Alps to Julius Caesar on the banks of the Rubicon and the Ides of March. Only when set within their wider historical context can these events and their participants come alive, and that is what this book seeks to achieve.

Chapter 1 looks back through the mists of time to the origins of Rome. Roman legends paint a vivid picture of the foundation of the city and of the kings who ruled before the expulsion of the monarchy and the creation of the Republic. Whatever the truth of those legends, they reveal how the Romans understood their past and the world in which the Republic emerged. Chapter 2 continues the story as the political structures of the Republic took shape and Rome established itself as the dominant power of the Italian peninsula. The unique Republican constitution was one of Rome's greatest strengths and a source of much admiration in later centuries. But the rise of Rome was no less due to forces from within Roman society, reflected in the roles expected of Roman men and women and the social and religious principles that governed their lives. This is the subject of Chapter 3. Only by exploring the Romans' own values and beliefs is it possible to understand the Republic's dramatic rise and fall.

Chapters 4 and 5 take up Rome's transformation from an Italian city-state into the mistress of an empire. The epic clash between Rome and Carthage for dominance in the western Mediterranean was fought out across three destructive Punic Wars, in which even Hannibal's genius could not save the Carthaginians. Rome's eventual triumph in turn drew the Romans into the complex Greek-speaking world of the eastern Mediterranean. Victory over the successor kingdoms to Alexander the Great raised Rome to new heights, and allowed Greek influences to spread throughout Roman society. The expansion of Rome, however, came at a cost. Chapter 6 explores the consequences of expansion for the Republic, and the crises of the 2nd century that marked the beginning of the end.

There was far more to the Roman Republic than politics and the might of the legions. Chapter 7 turns to the Republic's literature and art, from the words of Plautus, Catullus, and Cicero to the monuments of Rome, and the images from Republican times preserved in the doomed city of Pompeii. Yet as Republican culture reached its zenith, the Republic's days were numbered. The rise of the warlords described in Chapter 8 plunged the Republic into an escalating sequence of civil wars, from which Gaius Julius Caesar emerged triumphant. The murder of Caesar on the Ides of March 44 BC only brought further violence, until finally the Republic disappeared, replaced by the Roman Empire under the sole rule of Caesar's adopted son, the emperor Augustus. Even then, the Republic's legacy endured. In Chapter 9, that legacy is traced through the Roman Empire and the early Christian Church to the Renaissance of Machiavelli and Shakespeare and the 18th-century revolutions in the United States and France. Still to this day, the Roman Republic compels our fascination and pervades Western culture, offering to the present both an ideal and a warning.

Chapter 1
The mists of the past

According to legend, the story of Rome begins with the fall of Troy. When the Greeks poured forth from the Wooden Horse and brought the ten years of the Trojan War to an end, the Trojan prince Aeneas gathered around him the last survivors of the burning city. Under his leadership, the refugees from Troy sailed first to Carthage in North Africa and then to Italy, where they settled on the plains of Latium. Aeneas, the son of Venus, the goddess of love, did not actually found Rome. But his son Iulus Ascanius became the king of the Latin city of Alba Longa and the ancestor of the Julian clan, from whose ranks would later arise Julius Caesar and the emperor Augustus.

The descendants of Iulus Ascanius ruled Alba Longa for many generations. Then a discontented prince, Amulius, deposed his older brother Numitor and seized power. Numitor's sons were executed and his daughter, Rhea Silvia, was made a Vestal, a virgin dedicated to Vesta, the goddess of the hearth. Fate, however, intervened. The virgin Rhea was raped and gave birth to twin sons, whose father she believed was Mars, the god of war. Abandoned beside the River Tiber by their great-uncle, the twins Romulus and Remus were suckled by a she-wolf and raised by the king's herdsman. Upon reaching manhood, the brothers overthrew Amulius and restored their grandfather to power. They then returned to the site of their abandonment by the Tiber to

1. **Bronze wolf (possibly of Etruscan origin), with the children below added by a 15th-century pope**

found a new settlement on the Palatine Hill. Sibling rivalry swiftly came to a head. Unable to agree upon who would lead the emerging community, the twins turned to violence and Remus was killed. From that bloodshed the state that would rule the Mediterranean world was born. In 753 BC, on the traditional reckoning, Romulus gave his name to the city he had founded and became the first king of Rome.

The new settlement faced immediate social crisis. In order for his community to grow Romulus welcomed all who came to him, among them slaves, fugitives, and brigands. But Rome lacked sufficient women to provide the next generation. A solution had to be found. The Romans held a great festival to which they invited the nearby tribes, of whom the most prominent were the Sabines. At a chosen moment, the Roman men sprang out and seized every young woman they could catch. By the time the Sabines had prepared their counter-strike, those women were wives and mothers. Separating the armies, they demanded that their fathers and husbands make peace. The 'Rape of the Sabine Women' secured the future of the Roman community and began Rome's influence over its neighbours.

In Roman tradition, Romulus was the first of seven kings who successively ruled Rome for almost two and a half centuries. Romulus himself disappeared under mysterious circumstances during a storm, and was said to have ascended to the heavens as the god Quirinus. His successor, Numa Pompilius, was a Sabine. He was credited with the organization of the Roman calendar and of the most ancient rites of Roman religion. By contrast, the third king, Tullus Hostilius, was a warrior. During his reign the Romans destroyed their ancestral city of Alba Longa, of which only the temples were spared. Ancus Marcius, the fourth king, was the grandson of Numa, and like his grandfather placed great importance on the correct conduct of public religion. But he was also a warrior, who established the rituals by which Rome might justly go to war and defeated the surrounding Latin peoples. On Ancus' death power passed to Lucius Tarquinius Priscus, who had come to Rome from the Etruscan people to the north. His reign saw the expansion of the Roman city, particularly around the central Forum, and he laid the foundations for the great Temple of Jupiter on the Capitol above the Forum. These civic works were continued by the sixth king, Servius Tullius, Tarquin's son-in-law, who devised the census by which the Roman population was mustered and defined the city by the erection of the Servian Wall.

The seventh and last king of Rome was Lucius Tarquinius Superbus, 'Tarquin the Proud'. The son of Tarquinius Priscus and married to Servius' daughter, Tarquin overthrew Servius and seized power. He ruled by fear as a tyrant and ignored the Senate, whose role was to advise the king. Tarquin's sons shared their father's character, and from their crimes came the downfall of the monarchy and the creation of the Republic. At a drinking party outside Rome, the princes and their guests began to boast of the qualities of their wives. When they rode home to determine the truth, the princes discovered their own wives enjoying themselves in luxury. Lucretia, the wife of their friend Collatinus, was on the contrary the model of female virtue and was found spinning and directing the domestic servants. Her beauty aroused the lust of Sextus Tarquinius, the youngest prince, who returned in secret and raped her at sword point. Innocent of guilt, Lucretia nevertheless sought atonement and before her father and husband she drove a knife into her heart. The man who drew forth the knife was Lucius Junius Brutus, the ancestor of the conspirator against Julius Caesar. Rallying the Roman people, Brutus expelled Tarquin and his sons. In 510 BC, the Roman monarchy was dissolved. The kings were replaced by two elected consuls, of whom the first were Collatinus and Brutus, and the Roman Republic was formed.

From myth to history

What truths lie hidden within these legends of the ancient Roman past? No written sources survive from the centuries before the Republic's foundation. The story of the Trojan prince Aeneas was immortalized in the *Aeneid* of Virgil (70–19 BC), an epic poem composed over a thousand years after the estimated date of the sack of Troy. For Romulus and his successors, our most valuable account was composed by one of Virgil's contemporaries, far removed once again from the age of the kings. The historian Livy (59 BC–AD 17) concluded Book 1 of the 142 books of his *History of Rome* with the Rape of Lucretia and the expulsion of the Tarquins. Virgil and Livy lived through the Republic's final collapse and the rise of Augustus (31 BC–AD 14), the first Roman emperor. Their writings can hardly provide an accurate record of the distant centuries before the monarchy's fall.

This should not deny the importance of Roman tradition. The early years of Rome were held up by later generations as a golden age in which the structures of Roman society were laid down and the virtues which made Rome great were revealed. Important customs and practices were associated with the early kings, and heroes of the past established models for true Roman behaviour. Lucretia set the pattern for Roman women in the domestic sphere and defended her honour with her life. Brutus' liberation of Rome from Tarquin's tyranny drove his distant descendant to conspire against the dictatorship of Caesar. These models were more than rhetorical ideals. They influenced how later Roman men and women acted, and they reveal how the Romans themselves envisioned where they came from. The stories from the mists of the Roman past are crucial to our understanding of the Republic, even if they do not always shed light on Rome's historical origins.

In the absence of reliable literary sources, the modern historian of early Rome must turn to other forms of evidence and place the first Romans within their physical and cultural setting. Rome is located in the fertile plain of Latium which lies halfway down Italy's western coast. Italian geography is dominated by the Alpine mountains and the Po River valley to the north and by the Apennine range, which runs like a backbone down Italy. The Apennines are steeper and closer to the coast in the east than the west, and the majority of the fertile soil in central Italy is on the western side. The plain of Latium could support a dense farming population, although the land had to be defended from the raids of the hill people of the Apennines, of whom the most notable in early Roman history were the Samnites.

The Indo-European Italic people who would become known as the Latins occupied the plain of Latium in c. 1500–1000 BC. For these early arrivals, Rome was a natural site for settlement. A ring of seven hills offered defensive protection, and nearby lay the Insula Tiberina, the island that marked the easiest point at which the River Tiber could be crossed. To the north was the region of

Map 1. Early Rome and Italy

Etruria, which by approximately 900 BC had been settled by the
people known as the Etruscans. To the south from 750 BC onwards
were a number of cities founded by colonists from the Greek
world, including Syracuse in Sicily and Neapolis ('New City',
Naples), from whom southern Italy would take the name Magna
Graecia ('Greater Greece'). Latium in central-western Italy was at
the natural junction for land communication between Etruria and
Magna Graecia. This interaction of cultures was to exert a major
influence on early Rome.

Archaeology has revealed a human presence in the area of Rome in the Bronze Age (before 1000 BC). The first significant settlement on the Palatine Hill is then attested by Iron-Age huts from the 8th century, suggesting that the traditional Roman foundation date of 753 may be more accurate than we might have assumed. During the 7th century this initial Palatine settlement united with settlements on the other hills, and the urban landscape of Rome began to emerge. The causes of this crucial development are only hinted at in our literary record. One striking feature of the legendary seven kings of Rome is that the names of two of the later kings, Lucius Tarquinius Priscus and Lucius Tarquinius Superbus, are not Latin but Etruscan. The transformation of the scattered hill settlements into the city of Rome would appear to have taken place under Etruscan rule.

Who were the Etruscans? This is a question that scholars have debated for centuries. Their origins are unknown, but the Etruscans had settled northwest of Rome in what is now Tuscany by at least 900 and perhaps as early as 1200 BC. Thousands of Etruscan inscriptions have been found, but frustratingly they cannot be read, for the Etruscans were not an Indo-European people and their language has no surviving parallel. Our knowledge of Etruscan culture derives from archaeology, particularly the elaborate *necropoleis* (cities of the dead) around their towns. Magnificent tomb paintings depict feasting, dancing, and athletic contests, including gladiatorial combats, which formed part of Etruscan funerary rites. Their surviving art and craftwork drew extensively on Greek influences, and it was through the Etruscans that Greek culture first entered Rome.

The Etruscan influence upon early Rome was profound. The very name Roma (Ruma) may be Etruscan, and the city that emerged in the 6th century followed an Etruscan pattern. At the city's heart on the Capitoline Hill stood the greatest temple of Rome, dedicated to the triad of Jupiter, Juno, and Minerva. In Roman tradition the temple was begun by the Etruscan Lucius Tarquinius

Priscus, and the Capitoline triad recalls the Etruscan divine trinity of Tini, Uni, and Menvra. The urban layout of Rome imitated the grid pattern typical of Etruscan towns, and Roman houses again followed an Etruscan model with an *atrium* (open court) leading into the *triclinium* (banqueting hall) from which doors opened into sleeping quarters. Etruscan architectural designs also left their mark. Aqueducts and bridges, drainage systems, and the extensive use of arches and vaults were all Etruscan features which were to become characteristic of Roman architecture.

Nor was Etruscan influence limited to Rome's physical appearance. As Roman tradition acknowledged, a number of Roman religious practices were derived from the Etruscans, including divination through haruspicy, seeking the gods' will by inspecting the organs of sacrificial animals. It is possible that the gladiatorial contests so popular in Rome were inspired by Etruscan funeral games. The Roman Republic also drew on the Etruscans for symbols of authority. Livy attributed to the Etruscans both the *toga praetexta* (a white toga with a broad purple border) that senior Roman magistrates wore and the curule chair (*sella curulis*) in which the magistrates sat when performing their duties. The *fasces*, bundles of rods within which was bound an axe, were originally carried by the 12 lictors who accompanied Etruscan kings as attendants and bodyguards, and under the Republic the same honour was paid to each of the consuls.

By the late 6th century the Etruscans had become the dominant force in northern and central Italy. Despite the scale of Etruscan influence, however, Rome never became an Etruscan city. As the Romans would repeatedly demonstrate, it was a cardinal gift of the Roman genius to absorb and adapt the strengths of those they encountered without sacrificing their own identity. The Etruscans, like the Greeks in later centuries, contributed greatly to Roman culture yet ultimately fell under Roman dominion. The expulsion of the kings did not end Etruscan influence but reaffirmed Rome's political independence and began its slow rise to power. The Republic that now took shape was a uniquely Roman creation.

Chapter 2
The Republic takes shape

The Roman Republic did not come into existence overnight. Tarquin Superbus' expulsion in 510 BC only marked the first step on the long and winding path that led Rome to greatness. The centuries that followed were years of intense external and internal conflict. In this crucible the Republic was forged. Gradually, Rome conquered its region of Italy and began to extend its reach further afield. The unique political and social structures of the Republic took shape and created a force the like of which the ancient world had never seen.

Our knowledge of the Republic's formative years is greater than for the legendary kings but still far from extensive. More than 200 years separated the monarchy's fall from the Pyrrhic War (280–275 BC) which confirmed Roman control over central and southern Italy. Livy's *History of Rome* offers a confusing story of near-constant warfare and internal strife, and earlier records were lost when a Gallic warband sacked Rome itself in c. 387 BC. Yet the essential narrative is reasonably clear. Between 510 and 275 BC, Rome became the dominant power of the Italian peninsula. Roman rule united the Italian peoples, from the Etruscans to the north to the Greek city-states in the south, in an expanding web of alliances that played a fundamental part in Roman success. Rome's external expansion was inseparably intertwined with developments inside its borders. During these same years, Roman society and politics were transformed through a series of crises traditionally known as the Conflict of the Orders. By the early 3rd century, the Conflict had resolved into the characteristic structures that defined the Republic under the collective leadership of the *senatus populusque Romanus (SPQR)*: the Senate and People of Rome.

The conquest of Italy

The Romans had first begun to exert authority over the surrounding Latin peoples under the Etruscan kings. The overthrow of the monarchy inspired a reaction against the nascent Republic. A coalition of towns formed the Latin League, whose army was joined by the exiled Tarquins. Early in the 5th century BC, perhaps in 499 or 496, the Romans faced off against the Latin army at Lake Regillus near Tusculum. The struggle was fierce, and legend attributed Rome's final victory to the aid of the divine Dioscuri (Castor and Pollux, the twin brothers of Helen of Troy) who appeared as young horsemen and rallied the Roman troops. Victory established the military superiority of the Republic over its immediate neighbours and laid the foundation for the unification of Latium.

The network of alliances that Rome created with the Latins over the two centuries that followed the Battle of Lake Regillus marked a key step in the Republic's rise to power. As allies of Rome, each Latin town did not pay tribute but was required to provide a fixed number of soldiers who served in the Roman army under Roman generals. The Latins were entitled to a fair share of any plunder gained in war and were promised the protection of Rome against outside aggressors. The Latin allies were also integrated more closely into Roman society. Romans and Latins could contract valid economic agreements that were legally binding on both parties, and they could inter-marry without the children being regarded as illegitimate.

It is difficult to convey just how revolutionary the Roman–Latin alliance was by the standards of antiquity. The contemporary world of ancient Greece was dominated by individual city-states, fiercely independent and jealous of their rights. Seen in these terms, the relationship between the Republic and its Latin allies was one of remarkable sophistication. The Latins dramatically increased the population base and military power that Rome commanded, and so enabled Rome to transcend the limitations of a city-state in a way that Greek *poleis* like Athens and Sparta would never achieve. The privileges that Rome offered were attractive and so its superiority rested on consensus more than oppression, and in later centuries the Latin allies largely stayed loyal despite the pressures of expansion and Hannibal's invasion of Italy. As Rome did not require financial tribute from its allies, however, its superiority was only explicit in times of war when the allied contingents were summoned for the army. The need to assert this superiority, as well as to fulfil its promise to protect its allies, would help to drive Roman aggression throughout Republican history.

Even with the aid of its Latin allies, the Republic initially struggled to impose Roman authority beyond the region of Latium. A century of conflict saw Rome slowly gain the upper hand within central Italy, but then disaster struck. In 390 BC (the traditional date), or more probably 387, an army of Gallic raiders swept down from the north. The Gauls passed through Etruria, defeated a Roman army, and closed on Rome. The last defenders held out on the Capitoline Hill but the city fell to the invaders, an event that would not occur again for eight centuries until Alaric and the Goths entered Christian Rome in AD 410.

The Gallic Sack of Rome is one of the most famous episodes of early Roman history, and stories from the disaster passed into legend. Livy recounts how the senators remained seated in their houses like statues, until an awestruck Gaul touched one noble's beard. The noble brought his ivory staff down on the barbarian's head, and the senators were butchered where they sat. The Citadel on the Capitol would have fallen to a night assault had not the sacred geese of Juno raised the alarm, and the Senate even debated abandoning the site of Rome until a centurion nearby was heard to tell his men 'we might as well stop here', a remark heralded as a divine omen.

In truth, the significance of the Sack of Rome has almost certainly been exaggerated. The disaster had an undoubted psychological impact, reflected in the Roman hatred of Gauls still apparent over 300 years later in Caesar's Gallic Wars. But archaeology has revealed few traces of destruction, and the Sack does not appear to have undermined Roman power. The Republic revived swiftly, and to deter future invaders the city was defended by the Servian Wall later ascribed to the penultimate king Servius Tullius. The remainder of the 4th century BC saw ongoing Roman advances, now directed particularly towards southern Italy. It was here that the Romans encountered their greatest Italian rivals: the Samnites.

The Samnites were a tough hill people of the Apennine mountain range. In the 5th century BC they had moved into the plain of Campania and captured the originally Etruscan city of Capua. Roman expansion south towards Campania sparked tensions and three Samnite wars. The first war (343–341 BC) was little more than a minor skirmish, but had one major consequence. In 338 BC Capua signed a treaty with Rome. This marked an extension of Rome's allied network beyond the region of Latium, and the rights granted differed slightly from those offered to the Latins. Capua and Rome's other Italian allies again had to provide men for military service in return for Roman protection and a share of the plunder, but also had to pay a set annual tribute and received fewer civic privileges. Rome's relationship with its Italian allies further increased its resource base and army strength, although the restrictions placed on the Italians led to tensions which exploded into war in the last century of the Republic.

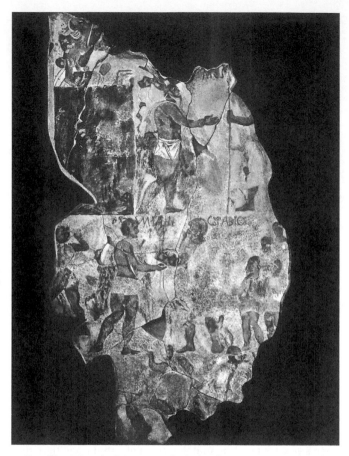

2. Esquiline Historical Fragment depicting the Roman general Fabius meeting the Samnite chieftain Fannius

Rome's rivalry with the Samnites came to a head in the second Samnite War (327–304 BC). A Roman attack led to humiliating defeat at the Caudine Forks in 321 BC, after which the defeated Roman army was forced to march under a yoke as a token of submission. Defeat only hardened Republican resolve. The secret of Roman success lay not just in its military might but perhaps even more in Rome's conviction of its own destiny and refusal to back down. In a pattern that would be repeated many times in the future, Rome regrouped its forces and returned to exact revenge. Unable to resist Rome alone, the Samnites formed a coalition with Gauls, Etruscans, and other Italians in a final attempt to oppose the spread of Roman dominion. At the Battle of Sentinum in 295 BC, Rome and its allies crushed the coalition and confirmed the Republic as the chief power of the Italian peninsula.

The last enemy whom the Republic faced during its conquest of Italy posed a very different challenge. Rome's expansion into southern Italy brought the Romans into closer contact with the Greek cities of Magna Graecia. Some of those cities welcomed Roman friendship, but amidst rising tensions the city of Tarentum looked to the east for aid in driving Rome back. The Tarentine appeal was answered in 280 BC by Pyrrhus, king of Epirus (modern Albania). Pyrrhus was one of a number of kings ruling the divided Greek-speaking eastern Mediterranean after the death of Alexander the Great in 323 BC. An ambitious man and an experienced soldier, Pyrrhus brought to Italy a powerful army of 20,000 infantry, 3,000 cavalry, and about 20 elephants, which Rome had never before encountered.

Pyrrhus' professional army was superior to anything in Roman experience. In the first two battles, at Heraclea in 280 BC and Asculum in 279 BC, the Romans suffered major defeats. But these Pyrrhic victories came at a high cost. The Battle of Asculum in particular left much of Pyrrhus' elite infantry dead on the field, inspiring his grim remark: 'One more victory like that over the Romans will destroy us completely.' The ferocity of Roman resistance caused Pyrrhus to withdraw to Sicily, and when he returned to Italy in 275 BC he was finally defeated by the Romans at Beneventum. Pyrrhus abandoned Italy (he was later killed in Greece attacking Argos after an old woman threw a roof tile at his head), and Tarentum surrendered. By 270 BC all of Magna Graecia had been incorporated within the Roman alliance, and Rome stood unchallenged as the mistress of Italy.

Senatus populusque Romanus

Throughout the years of Italian expansion, the social and political structures of the Republic continued to evolve. After the monarchy's fall, the ruling aristocracy of Rome was initially restricted to certain great families collectively known as the patricians (*patres*, 'fathers'). Only members of patrician families, such as the Claudii, Julii, and Cornelii, could hold religious or political office. All Roman citizens who were not patricians were classed as plebeians. While the plebeians did therefore include the poorest citizens, the plebeians were not simply 'the poor' as opposed to the patrician 'rich'. Some wealthy plebeians owned as much land as any patrician, but because they did not come from a patrician family they were excluded from holding office. Tension between patricians and plebeians was inevitable. The earliest disputes arose in reaction to patrician exploitation of the plebeian population. Over time, wealthier plebeians also sought to rally the wider plebeian body to support their claims to an equal share of political power. The long plebeian struggle for social and political rights has become known as the Conflict of the Orders.

Less than 20 years after the Republic's creation, if we are to believe the chronology of our sources, the Conflict of the Orders began. In 494 BC opposition arose against patrician treatment of plebeians who fell into debt. The poorer plebeians provided the bulk of the Republican army, and while on military service they struggled to maintain the farms from which they derived their livelihood. Many turned to patricians for aid, which left them open to abuse and even enslavement by their creditors. As the patricians controlled Roman politics, the plebeians found no help from within the existing system. Their solution was to go on strike. When the army was ordered out in 494 BC, the plebeians instead gathered outside Rome and refused to move until the patricians gave them some form of representation. This was the First Secession of the Plebs. Forced to make concessions, the patricians gave the plebeians the right to meet in their own assembly, the *Concilium Plebis*, and to elect their own officials to protect their rights, the tribunes of the plebs.

A second flash-point arose over patrician control of the law. Early Rome had no written legal code. Questions of justice were decided by customary unwritten law, preserved and judged by the patricians. Like debt-enslavement, this left the plebeians vulnerable to patrician abuse despite the protection provided by the tribunes. In c. 450 BC opposition to this arbitrary patrician justice led to the composition of the Twelve Tables, the first recorded Roman laws. Henceforth, plebeians could at least know the law, and their position gradually strengthened. By the end of the 4th century, the enslavement of Roman citizens for debt had been banned and all citizens possessed the right of *provocatio ad populum*, the right of appeal to the whole people against decisions made by a magistrate. This culminated in 287 BC with the *Lex Hortensia*, a law which declared that a plebiscite, a decree passed by the *Concilium Plebis*, was binding on the entire population, including patricians.

In the course of the Conflict of the Orders, the Roman people thus secured a degree of protection and of participation in the activity of the state. For the wealthier plebeians, this was not enough. They demanded a greater role and challenged the patrician monopoly on positions of power. Once again, the patricians were forced to make concessions. After more than a century of ongoing tensions, a law was passed in 367 BC allowing plebeians to stand for election as consul. The first plebeian consul was elected the following year, and from 342 BC onwards one of the two consuls had to be plebeian. Eventually, plebeians gained access to almost all major political and religious offices. The distinction between patricians and plebeians by birth still existed, but the Republic's ruling class had widened and a new aristocracy had emerged which contained both patrician and plebeian nobles. By the early 3rd century, this combined nobility was firmly established. So too were the three key elements that comprised the unique government structure of the Roman Republic: the magistrates, the Senate, and the popular assemblies.

The magistrates were the officials elected annually from the nobility to run the daily business of government. First and foremost were the two consuls who held the *imperium* (executive power) once wielded by the king. During their year in office, the consuls were the political and military heads of the state. They presided over the Senate, proposed laws if required, and commanded armies in the field. The consulship was usually the pinnacle of a Roman noble's career, and the Roman calendar dated each year by the names of those who held this highest office. The hatred of autocracy that had inspired the expulsion of Tarquin Superbus, however, remained strong. The election of two consuls prevented any one man from having too much power, and the consulship was held only for a single year.

Below the consuls were lesser magistrates, again elected annually. The major offices were those of praetor, aedile, quaestor, and tribune of the plebs. The praetor was the only magistrate apart from the consul to hold *imperium*, the right to command armies and preside over the Senate. The authority of the praetor was inferior to that of the consul, and the praetor's main role was civil and later provincial jurisdiction. Below the praetors were the aediles, who were responsible for the urban maintenance of Rome, including roads, water supply, food, and games. The most junior magistrates were the quaestors, who performed financial and legal duties. The exact roles and numbers of these three lesser magistracies expanded over time as the growth of Roman power increased the burden on the Roman state.

Tribunes of the plebs differed somewhat from the other magistrates. The office of tribune appeared after the First

Secession of the Plebs in 494 BC and was originally the only office open to wealthy plebeians. Ten tribunes were elected each year, and their intended role was to defend plebeians from unjust actions by patrician magistrates. For this reason the tribunes held considerable powers, including the right to intervene in support of a citizen being arrested by a magistrate, the right to veto the action of another magistrate, and the right to propose legislation in the *Concilium Plebis*. In theory the person of a tribune was sacrosanct, although this did not always protect those who used the office to pursue radical policies, most famously the Gracchi brothers in the 2nd century.

The other slightly unusual office was that of censor. Two censors were elected approximately every five years, but they held office only until they had completed their functions and never for longer than 18 months. Their primary role was to revise the list of citizens and assess both their property and their morality. This duty included a review of the Senate, into which they could enrol new members and remove any found guilty of improper behaviour. The censorship was therefore a prestigious office and was almost invariably held by ex-consuls. The most notorious censor of the Republican period was Cato the Elder (also known as Cato the Censor), who held the office in 184 BC. Cato strongly believed that the Republic of his day was declining from the moral standards of the early Romans. As censor he expelled from the Senate those whom he regarded as flouting traditional Roman behaviour, condemning one senator who had embraced his wife by daylight in the presence of their daughter.

These offices together formed the *cursus honorum*, the sequence of magistracies that a leading Roman noble might hold. In a conventional career, a man held his first office as a quaestor at a minimum age of around 28. He then became either an aedile or a tribune of the plebs, before seeking election as praetor. Those of sufficient renown could then aspire to the consulship and later perhaps stand as censor. A gap of two years was expected between

3. Census scene from the so-called 'Altar of Domitius Ahenobarbus' (actually a statue base) from the early 1st century BC

the possession of each office, and in the 1st century, when age requirements were imposed for the major magistracies, they were set at 39 for praetor and 42 for consul. These expectations could not always be enforced. Competition among the elite for office was intense, and exceptional individuals repeatedly challenged the *status quo*. Only in the last century of the Republic, however, did individuals emerge with sufficient power to dominate the highest offices and threaten the very basis of the Republican system.

All Republican magistracies shared certain key characteristics that reflected the Roman desire to check individual power. Office had to be earned through election, occupied for a limited period, and exercised together with one or more colleagues. There were certain exceptions to these rules. A consul or praetor at the end of their year in office could be granted an extension of their *imperium* should the need arise. They then became pro-consuls and pro-praetors, although such extended authority became common only in the 1st century. The other great exception was the position of dictator. Despite the Roman hostility to autocracy, the Republic recognized that there were occasions when a single leader was required. In such an emergency, a dictator was appointed with superior *imperium* to oversee the state. A dictator could hold office only for six months or for the duration of the emergency, whichever was shorter. The 'perpetual dictatorship' later held by Julius Caesar was in Roman eyes a contradiction in terms, and a major cause of his murder.

The magistrates were the executive arm of the Republic, responsible for daily government and for political and military leadership. Yet true political power in the early Republic did not lie with the individual magistrates but with the collective authority of the Senate. A Roman noble held office only for short periods of time during his adult life, and the tradition of annually elected magistrates gave those in office limited experience. At times this proved a weakness, notably when consular generals faced professional soldiers like Pyrrhus and Hannibal. Magistrates were therefore expected to follow the guidance of the Senate, which had evolved from the noble council that had advised the kings. A magistrate was himself part of the Senate, and after his year in office resumed his role as a normal senator. Major decisions were always first debated in the Senate, and in particular the Senate oversaw foreign policy, civil administration, and finance. It was the Senate that was the real foundation of Republican government.

Decisions proposed by the Senate had to be confirmed by the third element of the Republican system, the popular assemblies. It was the assemblies that approved laws and elected all the annual magistrates. There were several different forms of public assembly in Rome, but the two most important under the Republic were the *Comitia Centuriata* and the *Concilium Plebis*. The *Comitia Centuriata* elected consuls and praetors and made declarations of war. The *Concilium Plebis* elected tribunes of the plebs and passed plebiscites proposed by the tribunes. Although these popular assemblies had theoretical sovereign power, in reality they too followed the guidance of the Senate. The magistrates who summoned the assemblies only brought before them issues that had been debated already by the Senate, and the assemblies almost invariably endorsed the Senate's decision. It was a sophisticated system that acknowledged the right of all citizens to have a say in government while in practice keeping control in the hands of the nobility. The Republic was governed by the Senate and People of Rome, very much in that order.

The Republican constitution was a uniquely Roman creation. The people had a degree of sovereign power, but Rome was not a democracy and was far less vulnerable to popular whims than classical Athens. The ruling patrician and plebeian aristocracy was clearly defined but nevertheless open to new blood, and possessed a practical flexibility that the equally militaristic Spartans lacked. The magistrates held executive authority in their year in office, but the limitation of annual elections and the collective leadership of the Senate prevented any one individual from seizing autocratic power. The Republic was a stable, conservative, yet adaptable form of government that provided the platform for Rome's rise to greatness. Driven by its competitive and warlike senatorial elite, Rome became the dominant power of Italy and the wider Mediterranean world. This was the Republic's triumph. It was also its downfall. For the conquest of an empire generated pressures that the structures of the Republic had never been intended to withstand.

Chapter 3
Men, women, and the gods

The Roman Republic was a living entity, a complex and dynamic world that evolved with time yet always remained distinctively Roman. The social structure was an ordered pyramid from the senatorial aristocracy at the peak to the smaller farmers and craftsmen and the numerous slaves who provided much of the workforce. But this structure was never rigid, and the ability of outstanding men outside the hereditary elite to advance themselves was one of Rome's great strengths. In daily life the fundamental unit was the family household, dominated in theory if not necessarily in practice by the patriarchal *paterfamilias*. Women played largely subordinate roles, although their importance in Roman history is hardly done justice by our male literary sources. Private and public spheres merged together at all levels of Roman society, united through the shared cultural and religious values that shaped Rome's sense of its own identity.

Dignitas and *gloria*

In the middle of the 5th century, the fledgling Republic found itself under attack from the neighbouring peoples of central Italy. The situation was critical and Rome appointed a dictator, Lucius Quinctius Cincinnatus. Livy takes up the tale:

Cincinnatus, the one man in whom Rome reposed all her hope of survival, was at that moment working a little three-acre farm (now known as the Quinctian meadow) west of the Tiber, just opposite the spot where the shipyards are today. A mission from the city found him at work on his land – digging a ditch, maybe, or ploughing. Greetings were exchanged, and he was asked – with a prayer for divine blessing on himself and his country – to put on his toga and hear the Senate's instructions. This naturally surprised him, and, asking if all were well, he told his wife Racilia to run to their cottage and fetch his toga. The toga was brought, and wiping the grimy sweat from his hands and face he put it on. At once the envoys from the city saluted him, with congratulations, as Dictator, invited him to enter Rome, and informed him of the terrible danger.

Cincinnatus entered Rome and accepted the dictatorship. He summoned all men of military age to gather with their equipment, marched out and won a great victory, and returned to Rome to celebrate his triumph. His chariot was preceded by the captured enemy commanders and followed by his soldiers with their booty. Cincinnatus then resigned his dictatorship. He had been in office for just 15 days.

Is the story true? It does not really matter. Lucius Quinctius Cincinnatus was remembered as a model of the ideal Roman. This leading man of his time was a farmer, who tended his small plot of land with his own hands. When he was approached by the Senate's envoys, he dressed correctly in his toga before receiving their instructions, wiping away the sweat before accepting their request. He won glory through his victories and celebrated in triumph. Then he laid down his power, for he cared more about the good of the state than about his personal prestige. Cincinnatus thus represented in one person all the virtues to which the later Romans attributed the Republic's rise to greatness. The early history of Rome is full of such heroic examples: the sacrifice of Lucretia, which inspired Lucius Junius Brutus to overthrow the monarchy; Publius Horatius Cocles, defending the bridge across

4. Modern statue of Cincinnatus from Cincinnati

the Tiber against the Etruscan king Lars Porsena; Gaius Fabricius, who fought against Pyrrhus but warned the king when Pyrrhus' physician offered to poison his master.

Through these stories, we gain a glimpse of how the Romans saw their ancestors and themselves. Early Rome was held up as a golden age, whose people embraced a simple lifestyle uncorrupted by excessive luxury. From this virtuous life, they won divine favour and drew the strength in adversity that gave Rome superiority over its neighbours. Later generations were taught to emulate and surpass their heroic forebears. It was this emulation that helped to drive the Republic's expansion, which brought wealth into Rome on a previously unimaginable scale. And as the Republic finally collapsed into chaos and civil war, it was moral decline and the loss of ancestral virtue that the Romans invoked to explain their fate.

The early Republic's greatest heroes came from the highest level of Roman society, the senatorial elite. Following the fall of the monarchy, membership of the Senate became the chief marker of social and political status in Rome. The most ancient families such as the Julii, Fabii, and Cornelii traced their descent back to the time of the kings and beyond, and formed a largely hereditary aristocracy prominent throughout Republican history. But the senatorial elite were not a closed caste and remained open to new blood. The Conflict of the Orders saw wealthy plebeians gain equality with the older patricians, and in later centuries a slow stream of outsiders gained senatorial standing. Such an individual was known as a *novus homo* or 'new man', the first of his family to enter the Senate or to reach the consulship, and these included the luminaries Cato the Elder, Gaius Marius, and Marcus Tullius Cicero.

The Roman Senate was in theory a body of equals, but there was nevertheless a hierarchy of honour within the elite. When the Senate met in debate, the first men to speak were the presiding consuls. They were followed by the most senior ex-consuls, then the praetors and ex-praetors, and on down the chain of seniority. Junior senators usually did not speak, and those who did almost invariably followed the guidance of their elders. The Senate was therefore a conservative body in which the oldest and most experienced men had a powerful influence. The leader of the Senate, the man who spoke first after the consuls, was known as the *princeps senatus*, the first among the equals of the Senate. Augustus would later adopt this title of *princeps* as befitting the first Roman emperor.

What determined a man's standing in the Senate was his *dignitas*. This complex concept, far more nuanced than the English word 'dignity', represented the sum of an individual's personal worth and the worth of his family. Those who had held higher offices, especially the consulship, had more *dignitas* than those who had not. Those whose ancestors had won fame inherited greater *dignitas*, and an individual's actions could in turn promote (or erode) his *dignitas* and that of his family. Above all, the single most important means through which a man could enhance his *dignitas* was by winning *gloria*. In Republican Rome, the highest form of *gloria* was achieved through war, through leading armies to victory. Every Roman noble sought *gloria* to increase his *dignitas* and surpass his rivals within the senatorial hierarchy.

The story of Cincinnatus encapsulated the ideal to which senators sought to aspire. When called to the dictatorship, Cincinnatus already possessed such *dignitas* that no one challenged his appointment. He then won further *gloria* through his victories, which was recognized when the Senate granted him a triumph. This was the highest accolade a successful Roman general could receive, the right to parade a victorious army through the city of Rome displaying the prisoners and booty captured on campaign. The triumphal procession began outside the city boundary on the *Campus Martius*, the Field of Mars. From there the route passed into Rome, down the Circus Maximus, and then up the *Via Sacra*

(Sacred Way) through the Forum, culminating at the Temple of
Jupiter Optimus Maximus on the Capitol where the general
offered sacrifice in thanks for the god's favour.

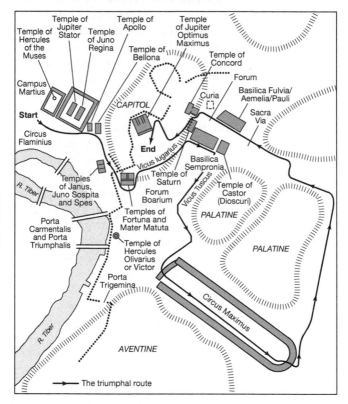

Map 2. The Triumphal Route through Rome

Each new senatorial generation was surrounded from childhood by
the stories of past heroes and monuments to their deeds. Even
within the home, famous ancestors watched over their descendants.
Pliny the Elder, writing in the early years of the Roman Empire,
described the images that stood in Republican noble houses:

They were not statues by foreign artists, not bronzes, not marbles, but wax masks (*imagines*) of members of their family, and these were displayed on individual urns so that their likenesses might be carried in procession at family funerals. For, invariably, when someone died, all the members of his family who had ever existed were present. The family tree was traced by lines connecting the painted portraits. Our ancestors' archive rooms were filled with books, records and written accounts of their achievements while in office. Outside the houses and round the door-lintels were other likenesses of those remarkable men. Spoils taken from the enemy were fastened to their doors and not even a subsequent purchaser of the house was allowed to take these down. Consequently, as they changed owners, houses celebrated an ongoing triumph.

It is impossible to exaggerate the significance for Republican history of the pressures placed upon the senatorial elite by the demands of *dignitas* and *gloria*. The men who dominated Roman social and political life were encouraged from birth to compete for prestige and to emulate and surpass the achievements of their ancestors. The impact this had in driving the military expansion of the Republic was a crucial factor in Rome's rise to power. Yet in the competitive ethos of the elite lay also the seeds for the Republic's fall. The desire for *dignitas* and *gloria* inspired all Republican champions, from Scipio Africanus the conqueror of Hannibal to Pompeius Magnus and Julius Caesar. As individual nobles acquired ever greater stature, they competed not only between themselves but with the collective authority of the Senate. Personal *dignitas* became more important than service to the state, until finally one man gained the power to subordinate Rome to his will.

Farmers, traders, and slaves

Below the senatorial aristocracy, Roman social divisions were less clear cut. In the late Republic, a bloc emerged directly below the senatorial elite known as the *equites* (equestrians or knights). They were heavily involved in trade and industry, which were of only limited importance in early Rome. But the main body of the free Roman population were small farmers who tilled their own fields and served when the army was called up to campaign. They were united with the elite through a bond essential to the harmony of Roman society, the relationship between patron and client. The patron offered protection and financial aid in return for the client's labour and political support through votes and public displays. It was an informal rather than legal relationship and so was open to abuse, but such abuse was rare. The support of numerous and loyal clients was important to a noble patron's *dignitas*, and the patron–client relationship provided one of the few forms of welfare available to the less fortunate in Rome.

During the great years of Mediterranean conquest, the small farmers provided the backbone of the Roman military. The early Republic did not have a permanent or professional army. Soldiers were called up when Rome was at war, which was admittedly frequent, and when not fighting had to maintain themselves on their farms. Those who had no property were not permitted to serve, initially because a soldier had to pay for his own equipment. As the military demands on Rome increased, pay for soldiers was introduced and the state took over the production of armour and weapons, which further ensured the uniform appearance and tactics of the army in the field. Yet the principle remained that only those who possessed a certain level of property should qualify for the *assidui*, those eligible for military service. This would change in the crises of the late Republic, a development that contributed directly to the Republic's fall.

The Roman population also included a significant number of non-citizens, which again increased as Rome's empire expanded. By far the largest and most important bloc were the slaves, who played a crucial role in Roman society and the economy. Slavery was endemic in the ancient world and was already firmly established in Rome when the Twelve Tables, Rome's first law code, were compiled in c. 450 BC. Male and female domestic servants performed many functions in noble households, from cooking and cleaning to teaching and entertainment, while in the countryside slaves farmed noble estates and laboured in state-run mines. In the early centuries slaves were usually prisoners from Rome's Italian wars, but as Roman power spread across the Mediterranean slave numbers skyrocketed: 150,000 slaves were taken from Epirus alone in 167 BC, and Julius Caesar enslaved 500,000 people or more in his campaigns in Gaul.

By comparison to slavery in more modern times, ethnicity does not appear to have greatly influenced Roman practice. There was no Roman equivalent to the later black slave trade to the Americas. Instead, certain peoples were valued for particular roles. The Greeks were prized as teachers and household servants, whereas Gauls and other 'barbarians' were preferred as farm labourers. Domestic workers were probably better off than those in the fields and the unfortunate slaves sent to work in the mines. Although their treatment could be brutal, however, Roman slaves had one unique advantage. Unlike the Greeks, the Romans allowed slaves who were freed to gain some (not all) of the benefits of citizenship. These *liberti*, freedmen, were expected to be loyal to their former masters, and under the Roman Empire some exceptional freedmen were to rise to positions of great wealth and power.

Amidst expansion and social change, the Roman economy remained fundamentally agricultural. For the vast majority of the population the chief concern was simply to grow sufficient food to eat, and even for the aristocracy land ownership was always the basis of wealth. Nevertheless, Rome's transformation into the mistress of a Mediterranean empire inevitably impacted dramatically on its economic life. This is reflected in the emergence of Roman coinage. Early Rome did not mint coins. Any agricultural surplus was exchanged through barter at temporary markets, with the only 'money' being bronze ingots that Rome began to issue at a fixed weight in the 4th century. Contact with the Greeks of southern Italy gradually encouraged Rome to adopt a more sophisticated currency. During the 3rd century Rome first minted its own bronze and silver coins, including the *as*, the *sestertius*, and the *denarius*. Roman minting multiplied in the 2nd century with the influx of precious metals, especially from the Spanish silver mines that Rome seized from Carthage, and by the last century BC Roman coinage was widespread across the Mediterranean world.

The need for a monetary economy reflected the growing demands on the Roman state and the rising importance of trade, both of which required more convenient means of exchange than barter. The state used coinage to pay the soldiers on campaign, a burden that grew with the empire. Taxation then recovered the coinage that the soldiers spent, creating the simple but effective basis for Roman currency circulation. The Roman road system in Italy and beyond, originally intended for military purposes, aided transportation of goods and people alike. Victory over Carthage in the 3rd century similarly gave Rome control over western seaborne trade and new access to eastern routes that extended as far as India and China. Much of this trade was in agricultural products, particularly grain imported from Sicily and North Africa to feed the city of Rome. But the most profitable was the import of luxury goods into Italy, from Greek art to Asian silk and spices. The increasing sophistication of the economy brought great benefits to the Republic. Yet those benefits mainly advantaged those who already had wealth to spend, and throughout Rome's history a large proportion of the population continued to depend upon subsistence agriculture.

Parents and children, husbands and wives

In the daily life of the Republic, as for almost all human societies, the fundamental social unit was the family. A microcosm of Rome itself, the Roman family reflected the principles that shaped Republican history. Roman names were statements of identity, above all for the senatorial aristocracy, while the traditional household roles of men and women reveal the patriarchal ideals of Roman society. The reality was slightly more complex, influenced by the essential factors of life expectancy, child mortality, and marital expectations. Physical setting also played a part. The Roman house, or *domus*, combined private and public space and set expectations for those who lived within.

Names held a special significance in a society where ancestry and inherited *dignitas* were key markers of social status. The tripartite names of the Republican male elite emphasized family rather than individual identity. A man's first name, or *praenomen*, such as Gaius or Marcus, was not distinctive and was used alone in conversation only by those closest to him. Fewer than 20 *praenomina* existed, and an oldest son usually had the same *praenomen* as his father. More important was the middle name, or *nomen gentile*, the name of a man's *gens* or clan. This name could be patrician (Julius, Fabius, Cornelius) or plebeian (Sempronius, Pompeius, Tullius) and was crucial to establishing a man's place in the social hierarchy. Different family branches within a given clan were then identified by a third name, the *cognomen*, which often began as individual nicknames. Thus the *cognomen* of Marcus Tullius Cicero originally meant 'chickpea', while the most famous bearer of the name Gaius Julius Caesar may have found his *cognomen* somewhat embarrassing ('Caesar' apparently indicated a thick head of hair, something the balding dictator lacked).

By contrast to men, naming patterns for women were much more straightforward. Women did not have a *praenomen* and rarely had a *cognomen*. A woman's name derived from the feminine form of her father's *nomen gentile*, and so Caesar's daughter was Julia and Cicero's Tullia. Elder and younger daughters were indicated by the addition of Major and Minor or by numbers (*prima, secunda*). A Roman's name therefore revealed his or her social standing, family history, and even whether he or she was the eldest child, while increasing the pressure to conform to the standards set by one's ancestors.

According to the Roman model for the ideal family, the head of a household was the *paterfamilias*, the oldest living male. As patriarch, the *paterfamilias* held *patria potestas* (paternal power) over his wife, their children, and their children's children. In theory at least, his legal authority was absolute. He arranged all marriages, determined whether infants were accepted or exposed to die, and could order even adult children be killed or enslaved without trial. In reality, fathers killing their sons was hardly normal and is known only from stories that were already notorious in Republican times. The few sources that provide glimpses of family life suggest a more complex and even loving environment, notably the letters of Cicero, whose wife Terentia (admittedly a famously strong-willed woman) ran their household and arranged their daughter Tullia's marriages. Cicero's relationship with Terentia was tense and ended in divorce, but he loved Tullia deeply, a reminder that behind the image of the austere *paterfamilias* Roman ideals still allowed for sentiment between parent and child.

The grim truths of life expectancy and child mortality also had a powerful impact upon the Roman vision of the family. Republican Rome was a pre-industrial society. The birth rate was high, perhaps 35 to 40 births per 1,000 people per year, but so too was the mortality rate. Average life expectancy at birth was under 30 and perhaps as low as 25. However, these figures were skewed by the high risk of child mortality, with some 50% of children dying before age 10. The exposure of unwanted girls added to the mortality rate, although how common this practice actually was is uncertain. Adults who survived to reach their 20s had an average life expectancy of around 55. Girls were usually first married by their late teens, men by their mid to late 20s.

This combination of low life expectancy with later marriage for men than for women had significant consequences. Women faced the risk of being widowed young by much older husbands, but men could be made widowers through women dying in childbirth. In addition, marriages among the elite were usually arranged for political reasons, and divorce and remarriage were frequent. Roman families therefore had to be flexible, with wide discrepancies in age and children of different parents within a single household equally possible. In 59 BC, as part of the agreement that formed the so-called First Triumvirate, Pompeius Magnus married Julia, the daughter of his fellow triumvir Julius Caesar. Pompeius was in his late 40s, six years older than his new father-in-law. He already had three children, and Julia was his fourth wife. She was probably in her teens and had never previously married. Against all the odds, the marriage proved a love match and helped to bind Pompeius and Caesar together, until Julia's death in childbirth in 54 BC.

The triumphs and tragedies of Republican upper-class family life took place in a setting that was itself uniquely Roman. The majority of Rome's urban population lived in multi-storey apartment buildings (*insulae*), of which only a few remains survive today. For the very rich, luxurious rural villas began to appear late in the Republican period and flourished under the Empire. But the characteristic domestic residence of the Republican elite was the *domus*. In the reception hall (*atrium*) and the adjoining rooms, the master of the house met his clients and dealt with political business. It was also here that family records were kept, the *imagines* of great ancestors looked down on their descendants, and offerings were made to the *lares familiares*, the protective spirits of the household. Towards the rear of the house were the banqueting hall (*triclinium*) and sleeping chambers (*cubicula*). Women were prominent in those rooms, but the Roman *domus* had no specifically gendered areas and there was no rigid separation between private and public

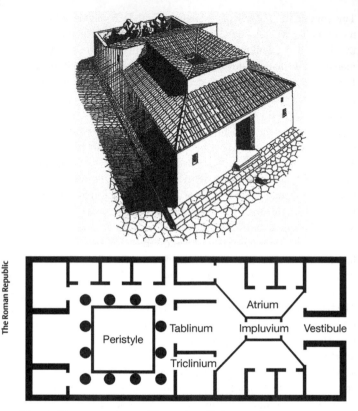

Map 3. Reconstruction and floor plan of a Roman *domus*

space. The *atrium* in particular stood in both worlds as a physical symbol of the privileges and responsibilities of the Roman elite.

Little has been said about the female half of the Roman population outside their roles as daughters and wives. The men who wrote our sources were more concerned with politics and warfare, and in their patriarchal vision of society the ideal woman was Lucretia, spinning as she waited for her husband's return.

Lucretia's sacrifice after her rape placed her family's honour above her own life. Four and a half centuries later Julius Caesar, one of the most notorious adulterers in Republican history, divorced his innocent wife after a dubious party because 'Caesar's wife must be above suspicion'. The women in these stories are placed firmly in a domestic setting, and judged less as individuals than by how their actions reflected upon their husbands.

Few public opportunities were open to Roman women under the Republic. They could not hold office or vote in the assemblies. Female intervention in politics was only acknowledged at moments of great crisis, such as the Rape of the Sabine Women in the legendary past. Almost the only public functions in which women did play a prominent part concerned religion. The Vestal Virgins, the most famous priestesses of Rome, predated the city itself, for Romulus' mother Rhea Silvia is said to have been a Vestal. These priestesses served Vesta, the goddess of the hearth, and their chief duty was to maintain the eternal fire on Vesta's altar. Girls from leading families were appointed Vestals when aged 6–10, and served for a minimum of 30 years. Some chose to serve for life, but former Vestals were eligible for marriage and widely respected. During their period of service, however, their vows were rigidly enforced. Vestals who allowed the sacred fire to die were scourged, while the penalty for loss of virginity was to be buried alive. In times of crisis the college of Vestals was often suspected of laxity bringing down divine wrath, and after the disastrous Battle of Cannae against Hannibal two Vestals were sentenced to burial (one committed suicide before the punishment could be carried out).

Yet Roman women deserved more than to be reduced to a few virgin priestesses and heroic archetypes. Women directed domestic and economic affairs in their households, overseeing cooking, clothing production, and childcare. Outside the elite, wives ran shops alongside their husbands and managed farms while their menfolk were away serving in ever longer and more distant wars. Senatorial ladies could be highly educated and they too shared the aristocratic concern for *dignitas* and emulation of the past, inspiring proper Roman behaviour in their children. Cornelia, the daughter of Hannibal's conqueror Scipio Africanus, is said to have driven her sons Tiberius and Gaius Gracchus into their doomed political campaigns through her repeated reproach that the Romans did not yet speak of her as the mother of the Gracchi. After their deaths, Cornelia was visited by many prestigious guests, from Roman nobles to reigning kings. 'What they admired most of all was to hear her speak of her sons without showing sorrow or shedding a tear, and recall their achievements and their fate to any inquirer, as though she were relating the history of the early days of Rome' (Plutarch).

An anonymous epitaph from the late 1st century, known as the *Laudatio Turiae*, speaks for all the forgotten women of the Republic. In this fragmentary inscription, a husband eulogizes his wife (possibly named Turia), who has died after four decades of marriage. Amidst the civil wars of the 1st century, she supported him when he was in exile and won clemency on his behalf from Caesar Augustus. She is praised for her loyalty and obedience, her industry and modesty. So great was her sense of duty that, when the marriage proved childless, she offered divorce to allow her husband to seek a more fertile partner. His response spoke volumes:

> To think that separation should be considered between us before fate had so ordained, to think that you had been able to conceive in your mind the idea that you might cease to be my wife while I was still alive, although you had been utterly faithful to me when I was exiled and practically dead! What desire, what need to have children could I have had that was so great that I should have broken faith for that reason and changed certainty for uncertainty? But no more about this! You remained with me as my wife, for I could not have given in to you without disgrace for me and unhappiness for us both...You deserved everything but it did not fall to my lot to give you everything as I ought. Your last wishes I have regarded as law; whatever it will be in my power to do in

addition, I shall do. I pray that your Di Manes will grant you rest and protection.

The *pax deorum*

The final crucial element that united Republican society was religion. In an uncertain world shaped by forces that the ancient Romans could neither understand nor control, faith in the gods offered a measure of reassurance and protection. Looking back, the historian Livy explained the rise of Rome less by the Republic's unique constitution and legionary might than by the divine favour that the early Romans won through their piety and morality. However alien Republican beliefs may seem to modern eyes, religion was an integral part of all aspects of Roman life. There were small household rituals that venerated the spirits that watched over the family, and great sacrifices and processions in honour of the highest deities who guarded the state. The gods' will was sought through the flight of birds and analysis of the entrails of sacrificial victims, and no election or declaration of war was undertaken without seeking divine approval.

In religion, as elsewhere, Rome drew inspiration from many sources. The highest gods and goddesses of Rome were the Olympians ruled by Jupiter (Zeus), whose worship was already firmly established in Rome when the Republic came into existence. Alongside the Olympians stood native Italian deities, from Quirinus, who came to be associated with the deified Romulus, to Janus, the two-faced god of doors, whose shrine near the Forum was only closed when all was at peace (a rite that allegedly occurred only twice in Rome's history before the reign of emperor Augustus). Rome 'herself' was revered as the personified Roma, while on a more personal scale stood the domestic shrines to the *lares* and *penates*, the guardians who watched over the home.

This diverse pantheon was always open to new arrivals. The absorption of foreign gods into Rome was a mark of superiority that also established bonds between the Romans and their conquered foes. From the Etruscans, the Romans derived the *haruspices*, diviners who examined the entrails of sacrificial animals. Spurinna, the soothsayer who warned Julius Caesar to 'beware the Ides of March', was a *haruspex*. The Sibylline Books, the most renowned oracle of Rome, were Greek verses acquired by the last king, Tarquin Superbus, from the Sibyl (prophetess) of Cumae. According to legend, the Sibyl offered Tarquin nine books of prophecies but the king refused to pay her price. The Sibyl burned three of the books and offered the remaining six at the same price, and when rejected again burned three more, until Tarquin submitted and bought the three surviving books. They were held in Jupiter's Temple on the Capitol and consulted only at moments of great crisis. It was on the command of the Sibylline Books that worship of Cybele, the Magna Mater (Great Mother), came to Rome from Asia Minor during the war with Hannibal. Her cult image (a meteorite) was installed in a new temple on the Palatine Hill as a guarantee of Roman victory over foreign invaders of Italy, although Roman citizens were barred from participation in Cybele's orgiastic rituals.

Roman religion was thus highly inclusive. The Romans did not impose their gods upon those they conquered, but incorporated the customs of defeated foes into their own cults. Yet we should avoid describing Roman religion as 'tolerant' in comparison to more exclusive monotheistic religions like Christianity and Islam. Tolerance implies a defined truth to which alternatives are then permitted to exist. Roman polytheism was neither tolerant nor intolerant, but absorbed the religious practices of others and offered no motive for persecution on specifically religious grounds. It is true that in 186 BC the Bacchanalia in honour of Dionysus was temporarily suppressed by order of the Senate. This was essentially a matter of public order, to check the drunken riots of Dionysus' followers, and worship of the god of wine continued in more acceptable forms. The Jews with

5. Cult of Dionysus, Villa of the Mysteries (Pompeii)

their unique religious identity likewise posed an exceptional challenge, but a Jewish community in Rome was firmly established by the last century of the Republic. Only under the Empire would major outbreaks of violence occur between Romans and Jews and between both groups and the newly emerging Christians.

The myriad cults of Rome each had their own traditional forms and rites. There was no expectation of uniformity, no holy text or creed that every Roman was expected to uphold. What bound the different elements together was the universal human need for guidance and security in a dangerous world. That need found expression through the fundamental Roman religious principle of the *pax deorum*, the 'peace of the gods'. The gods were powerful; they could also be terrible. Through correct ritual and prayer, the

43

Romans sought to maintain the gods' favour and placate their wrath. Individuals asked for divine protection during illness and childbirth, or for safety and prosperity at times of danger. Domestic sacrifices were offered for the well-being of the household; public festivals did the same on behalf of the state. To Romans like Livy, the disasters of the last century of the Republic could only be attributed to the loss of the morality and *pietas* that had once made Rome great.

Belief in the *pax deorum* and the essential importance of humanity's relationship with the divine underlay a number of characteristic features of Roman religion. In comparison to Christianity, which places more value upon individual piety and prayer, Roman religion was strongly communal. Personal expressions of belief were less significant than participation in shared rituals, from private household ceremonies to state festivals, which appealed to the gods for the collective good. For the same reason, great weight was placed upon the need to perform all rituals perfectly, without error or interruption. The slightest fault, a stutter in prayer or the misbehaviour of a sacrificial animal, required the entire ritual to be repeated. This obsession with formula and performance reflects the Roman emphasis on correct action (orthopraxy) rather than correct belief (orthodoxy) and to us may seem impersonal. But we would be wrong to dismiss the religion of the Romans as insincere. Roman tradition abounded with stories of what befell those who slighted the gods. Publius Claudius Pulcher, who commanded the Roman fleet at Drepana in 249 BC during the First Punic War with Carthage, ignored unfavourable omens when he went into battle. Informed that the sacred chickens had refused to eat, he threw the birds overboard saying 'let them drink'. His disastrous defeat ended Pulcher's political career, a fitting fate for one who had invited divine punishment.

Rituals were performed for the communal good, and it was therefore appropriate that those who conducted religious ceremonies were those who guided their communities in social and political affairs. Household rites were conducted by the *paterfamilias*, state rites by magistrates who also held priestly offices. Unlike many ancient cultures Rome thus had no distinct religious caste, and only a few priests and priestesses (among them the Vestal Virgins) had full-time duties. The vast majority of Roman priests were men from the senatorial elite for whom religious responsibilities were inseparable from their political careers. There were many different colleges of priests, from the *augurs* responsible for divination to the *decemviri sacris faciundis* ('the ten men for the performance of rites') who inspected the Sibylline Books when requested by the Senate. The highest priest was the *pontifex maximus*, the head of the college of *pontifices*, whose chief role was to oversee religious law and so preserve the *pax deorum*. Julius Caesar was *pontifex maximus* from 63 BC until his death in 44 BC, and after the Republic's fall the title passed to the emperors, who represented the state before gods and humans alike.

The close union between religion and politics in Rome has long worried modern observers who expect a clear separation between 'Church' and 'State'. Roman nobles certainly did manipulate religion for political ends. Marcus Calpurnius Bibulus opposed his fellow consul Julius Caesar in 59 BC by declaring that he was 'watching for omens', a religious claim that technically invalidated every action that Caesar took. Yet such apparently blatant manipulation could only be attempted because such questions mattered. An intellectual like Cicero could express scepticism about contemporary beliefs while still upholding veneration of the gods and the *pax deorum*. Roman attitudes towards religion may seem impersonal or political to our eyes, but this says more of our expectations than theirs. The countless gods, shrines, rituals, and festivals that made up the diverse world of Roman religion filled a very real need for centuries, and continued to do so long after the Republic itself disappeared.

Chapter 4
Carthage must be destroyed

By 275 BC the political and social structures that defined the Roman Republic were firmly established. The collective leadership of the Senate provided stability and channelled the ambitions of the aristocracy. Assemblies and elections gave the populace a voice, and the agricultural economy provided the manpower for Rome's armies. The Roman allied network, extending from the surrounding Latin peoples to the cities of Magna Graecia, increased the Republic's resource base and gave Rome control over central and southern Italy.

Yet the Republic was still no more than a regional power. Its influence was restricted to the Italian peninsula, and Rome played little role in wider Mediterranean affairs. During the 3rd century this changed. The broadening of Roman horizons beyond Italy brought Rome into direct conflict with the most dangerous enemy that the Republic would face, the North African city-state of Carthage. Their struggle for power between 264 and 146 BC brought Rome almost to its knees and inspired some of the greatest drama and heroes of Republican history. In the course of three 'Punic' Wars Carthage was finally destroyed, and Rome was transformed into a true Mediterranean power.

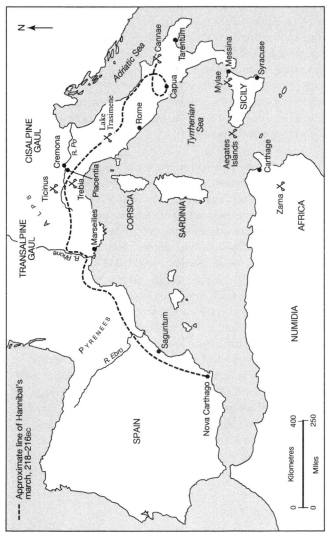

Map 4. The Carthaginian empire and the Punic Wars

History is written by the victors. Ancient Carthage has left few remains, and no Punic account of their long struggles with Rome survives. Our knowledge of Carthage and the Punic Wars derives chiefly from the Roman history of Livy and the pro-Roman Greek historian Polybius of Megalopolis. We therefore know all too little of the Carthaginians, and we view their motives and actions through the biased lens of their Roman foes. Nevertheless, it is possible to reconstruct the primary characteristics that defined Carthaginian society and made Carthage such a formidable rival to the rising Roman Republic.

Carthage was founded in c. 800 BC by colonists from the eastern city of Tyre in modern Lebanon. Its founders were Phoenicians (Latin *punici*), a maritime trading people, and Carthage stood on a superb natural harbour on the promontory of the present-day city of Tunis. Ideally situated to control trade in the western Mediterranean, Carthage established a commercial empire that extended across North Africa and into Spain, Sardinia, and Sicily. The wealth of Carthage was proverbial in antiquity, 'the richest city in the world' according to Polybius, and in contrast to Rome much of its population was devoted to trade and industry rather than agriculture. This was reflected in Carthage's political and military structure. Carthage was an oligarchy, ruled by the richest families. Its army was based on mercenaries under Carthaginian officers, including elite cavalry from Numidia, and the formidable if unreliable weapon of the now extinct North African elephant. More important to Carthage was its navy. Carthage maintained some 200 quinquiremes, oared galleys 45 metres long and equipped with a bronze-encased ram. Each ship required 300 rowers and could carry 120 marines for combat. Powerful and well drilled, the Carthaginian navy dominated the western Mediterranean in the years before the First Punic War.

The First Punic War

The rise of the Roman Republic put it on a collision course with Carthage. Early contact between the two states was relatively amicable, and during the Pyrrhic War Rome and Carthage signed a treaty allowing mutual cooperation against Pyrrhus' aggression. After Pyrrhus' defeat, however, Roman dominion over southern Italy drew Rome into the affairs of Sicily, which lay within the Carthaginian sphere of influence. Carthage had fought for centuries against the Greek cities of Sicily, of which the greatest was Syracuse. In 288 BC a band of Italian mercenaries calling themselves the Mamertines (the sons of Mars) seized the Sicilian city of Messina. Raiding Carthaginian and Syracusan territory indiscriminately, the Mamertines aroused hostility on all sides, and in 265 BC rival factions within Messina appealed to both Rome and Carthage for aid. The Carthaginians reacted first by sending a fleet, but a Roman army then crossed into Sicily and the Carthaginian commander surrendered the town (for which he was later crucified). Syracuse allied with Rome against Carthage, and in 264 BC the First Punic War began.

The Carthaginians had a long history of involvement in Sicily, and their response to the appeal from Messina is easy to understand. Why did Rome come to the Mamertines' aid? One motive was fear, for the Romans were concerned that Carthage might dominate Sicily and threaten Rome's hold on Italy. The Romans were also concerned to maintain the loyalty of their Italian allies. By aiding the Mamertines, Rome demonstrated that it would support its allies in times of danger and so confirmed its *fides* (good faith). Fear and *fides* were the motives that our Roman sources preferred to emphasize, for the Romans claimed that they waged war only in defence of themselves or their friends. These motives were genuine, but they do not tell the whole story. Roman society was geared towards warfare and the economic rewards of conquest, while the nobility competed for military *gloria*. It was the consuls who led the armies and the Senate in which all major decisions were debated, and it was the senatorial nobility who drove the Roman war effort.

After the initial conflict over Messina, the land war in Sicily soon ground to near stalemate. Carthage relied on defending the coastal towns. The Romans had little experience of siege warfare, and the Punic fleet kept the towns supplied and were even able to bring in elephants by sea. This stalemate, combined with recurring Carthaginian naval raids on the Italian coast, drove the Republic for the first time to construct a proper navy. Rome did already have a few ships, but its fleet was small and out of date compared to Carthage's state-of-the-art warships. Then a Carthaginian quinquireme ran aground, and in 60 days the Romans built 120 quinquiremes of their own, manning the ships with crews from their Greek allies in southern Italy.

Roman tradition may have exaggerated a little, but the creation of this fleet almost from nothing is among the most remarkable achievements of Republican history and a tribute to Roman organizational genius. To compensate for the superior skill and experience of the Carthaginians at sea, the Romans added to their ships the *corvus* ('crow'), a boarding ramp with an iron spike at the end to bind ships together and establish the fixed platform of a land battle. Armed with this weapon, the new Roman fleet won a major victory in 260 BC at Mylae. 50 Carthaginian ships were captured and their bronze beaks used to adorn a column in the Roman Forum in honour of commander Gaius Duilius.

The sudden emergence of Roman naval power altered the course of the war. Sensing their opportunity, the Romans used their fleet to send an army to Africa in 256–5 BC to threaten Carthage itself. However, the army was crushed by Carthaginian mercenaries led by the Spartan Xanthippus, and the Roman relief fleet was caught in a terrible storm – 280 ships were lost, with over 100,000 rowers and soldiers on board. A second fleet fell victim to a storm in 253 BC, in part because the *corvus* made the Roman ships more vulnerable in rough weather. Then in 249 BC the Carthaginians won a naval battle at Drepana, after the Roman commander Publius Claudius Pulcher invited divine wrath by throwing the sacred chickens overboard. Like the war on land, the war at sea had become a struggle of attrition, with neither side able to gain an advantage.

By the 240s the war was entering its third decade and both sides were exhausted. Perhaps 20% of Italian manpower had died in storms and battles, yet still the Republic refused to negotiate a peace. Rome dug deep. New taxes were raised and the nobility ordered compulsory loans from themselves, with every three senators responsible for providing a warship. Thus one more fleet was built. A final naval victory was won near the Aegates Islands off western Sicily in 241, and Carthage sued for peace.

Under the terms of the treaty, the defeated Carthaginians abandoned Sicily, though not their other possessions, and paid a heavy indemnity of 3,200 silver talents (approximately 100 tonnes). Bankrupt, Carthage immediately faced a massive mercenary revolt which lasted until 237. The Romans exploited their enemy's weakness by seizing Sardinia, and added insult to injury by threatening renewed war unless Carthage paid a further 1,200 talents in tribute. The Carthaginians had little choice except to submit, but Rome's high-handedness only increased their sense of grievance. Like the Treaty of Versailles 2,000 years later, the end of the First Punic War sowed the seeds for future conflict.

The First Punic War demonstrated the Republic's resilience under military and economic pressure and confirmed the loyalty of its allies under enormous strain. At the war's end, Sicily was taken as the first tribute-paying province of Rome. Unlike the Italian allies, Sicily received a praetor as a Roman governor, supported by a quaestor to oversee taxation and a small garrison. No additional bureaucracy was provided. Rome preferred to leave the existing social and political structures in place and govern through the local elites. It was a simple and flexible system which became the model for all Roman provincial administration under the Republic and was soon extended to Sardinia.

Hannibal and Scipio

In the aftermath of the loss of Sicily and then Sardinia, Carthage turned to its last remaining overseas possession in Spain. There it expanded its territory, exploiting the rich Spanish silver mines to pay the tribute that Rome demanded. The general commanding in Spain was Hamilcar Barca ('Thunderer'). Determined to restore Carthaginian pride and avenge its defeat, Hamilcar is said to have made his son swear at the age of 9 that he would always be the enemy of Rome. His son's name was Hannibal. The greatest single foe that the Roman Republic ever faced, and arguably the finest general of antiquity, Hannibal was immortalized by Livy:

> Under his leadership the men invariably showed to the best
> advantage both dash and confidence. Reckless in courting
> danger, he displayed superb tactical ability once it was upon him.
> Indefatigable both physically and mentally, he could endure with
> equal ease excessive heat or excessive cold; he ate and drank not to
> flatter his appetites but only so much as would sustain his bodily
> strength...Mounted or unmounted he was unequalled as a fighting
> man, always the first to attack, the last to leave the field. So much
> for his virtues – and they were great. But no less great were his
> faults. Inhuman cruelty, a more than Punic perfidy, a total disregard
> of truth, honour, and religion, of the sanctity of an oath, and of all
> that other men hold sacred.

It was Hannibal who led the Carthaginian forces into the Second Punic War. For Livy, the war's prime cause lay with Hannibal himself and the 'Barcid Vendetta' against Rome that he inherited from Hamilcar. The reality was more complex. Carthage's Spanish expansion alarmed Rome, and in c. 226 BC a treaty was signed that fixed the River Ebro in northern Spain as the boundary between their respective spheres. Yet Rome also established an alliance of friendship with the Spanish town of Saguntum, located 100 miles south of the Ebro deep inside the Carthaginian sphere. An attack upon that town by Hannibal in 219 BC provided Rome with a perfect *casus belli*, and after Carthage refused to surrender Hannibal for punishment, the Second Punic War began in 218 BC. Hannibal's actions were certainly provocative, but despite Rome's claim to be defending its ally, Rome too was eager to fight. So began 'the most memorable war in history' (Livy).

Rome had intended to fight on Carthaginian territory in Spain and North Africa. By the time that the Roman armies were prepared, however, Hannibal was already marching for the Alps. He was determined to attack the Roman strengths of manpower and resources directly by invading Italy, and so he abandoned his communications and risked the harsh crossing of the mountains. Over half his army and many of his elephants died in the Alpine passes, but Hannibal entered Italy with some 20,000 highly experienced Spanish and African infantry and 6,000 superb cavalry, much of it from Numidia. Cisalpine Gaul, the region of Italy just south of the Alps, had only been conquered by Rome in the years since the First Punic War. The local Gallic population revolted and joined Hannibal on his march south.

Hannibal's Numidian cavalry won an initial skirmish at the River Ticinus in November 218 BC, before the main Roman field army arrived under the consul Sempronius Longus. Confident of victory, the Romans attacked across the River Trebia on a bitterly cold morning in December 218 and were crushed, with the loss of over 20,000 men. Hannibal immediately released all his Italian prisoners without ransom, proclaiming the 'liberation' of Rome's allies. At this stage Hannibal's propaganda had little effect, and after waiting out the winter a second Roman army came to meet him under one of the newly elected consuls for 217, Gaius Flaminius. Pursuing Hannibal through Etruria, the Romans marched round the shores of Lake Trasimene and there fell straight into a trap. On a misty morning, Hannibal's Numidian cavalry cut off the Roman rear and 15,000 men were killed in battle or drowned, including Flaminius.

In this state of emergency Rome appointed a dictator, Quintus Fabius Maximus. Nicknamed Cunctator ('Delayer'), Fabius adopted a new strategy, avoiding open battle and seeking to grind Hannibal down. This un-Roman strategy was deeply unpopular, and Fabius was unable to prevent Hannibal slipping past him into southern Italy. New consuls were elected in 216, and Lucius Aemilius Paullus and Gaius Terentius Varro led the army to meet Hannibal on a flat plain at Cannae. Outnumbered by nearly two to one, Hannibal nevertheless managed to encircle the Romans, and they were trapped and butchered. Perhaps 50,000 Romans died, the greatest Republican defeat for over a century, and Hannibal advanced to within 6 miles of Rome.

The Battle of Cannae was the high watermark of Hannibal's success and secured his reputation as a military genius (his tactics are still taught in officer training courses to this day). For the first time his propaganda began to have an impact and he succeeded in winning over a number of Rome's allies, especially the Greek colonies in southern Italy and Syracuse in Sicily. But he was unable to attack Rome itself, whether from hesitation or because he lacked the resources to do so. Even after the Cannae disaster, the majority of Rome's Italian allies remained loyal. Hannibal had exposed the weakness in the Republican system of annual elected magistrates, and now Rome turned again to Fabius Maximus Cunctator, who was restored to power with the more aggressive Marcus Claudius Marcellus as his colleague. These two men, hailed as the 'Shield and Sword of Rome', oversaw the Roman recovery. In his great victories, Hannibal had killed over 70,000 Romans in just three years. By 212 there were 200,000 Roman soldiers in the field, in Italy, Sicily, and Spain. Some 50,000 men were deployed solely to watch the outnumbered Hannibal, never again offering battle but restricting his movements and crushing those who joined his side. The strain was colossal, but as in the First Punic War the Romans refused to back down.

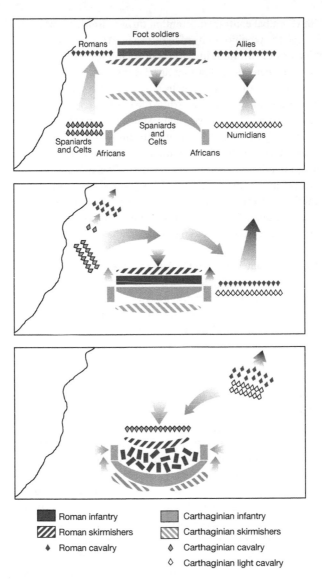

Roman infantry   Carthaginian infantry
Roman skirmishers   Carthaginian skirmishers
Roman cavalry   Carthaginian cavalry
   Carthaginian light cavalry

Map 5. Battle plan of Cannae

With Hannibal contained, attention turned elsewhere. Marcellus captured the rebellious city of Syracuse in 211, a siege made difficult by the brilliant inventions of Archimedes which reportedly included a claw that lifted Roman ships from the water and 'scorpions' that shot small iron darts. Archimedes was cut down by an unknown soldier when the city fell, a victory that secured Roman control over Sicily. Marcellus himself was later killed in Italy by another of Hannibal's ambushes in 208, and shortly afterwards the Carthaginians made their only significant attempt to reinforce Hannibal's army. That relief force was destroyed at the River Metaurus in 207, and the head of Hannibal's brother Hasdrubal was thrown into his camp. By this stage, the Italian theatre of war had almost become a sideshow. Decisive events were unfolding in Spain.

After Hannibal had crossed the Alps into Italy, the Roman generals Publius and Gnaeus Cornelius Scipio had launched a series of attacks upon Carthage's Spanish possessions. Then in 211 the two brothers were killed in battle. Their replacement, in an action unprecedented in Republican history, was Publius' 24-year-old son, another Publius Cornelius Scipio. The young Scipio had never held a position of authority and was not eligible for public office, but he was popular, brave, and a good soldier. Upon taking command, he immediately reorganized the army in Spain. He introduced the *gladius* (the Spanish shortsword) and the *pilum* (the heavy spear), and gave the Roman legion a more flexible formation based on maniples of 120 men drawn up in 3 lines totalling 4,200 men per legion. This flexible formation was highly suitable for the rough ground of Spain, and would later prove equally effective against the more rigid Greek phalanx. With his new army, Scipio crossed 250 miles in 5 days to launch a surprise attack upon the Carthaginian headquarters at Nova Carthago (modern Cartagena). Realizing that the town's defences were weak on the seaward side, Scipio crossed a lagoon at low tide and seized the city in 209. The fall of Nova Carthago gave Rome control of the rich silver mines nearby, and by 205 Carthage had been forced to withdraw from Spain.

Scipio returned to Rome to receive a hero's welcome in 205. Riding a wave of popular support, he then secured the consulship and command of the planned Roman invasion of North Africa over the objections of older, more conservative senators led by Fabius Maximus. The Roman landing forced Hannibal to return to defend Carthage itself, a city he had not seen in over 30 years. Scipio's diplomacy won the support of the Numidians, and at the Battle of Zama in 202 BC Hannibal lacked his usual superiority in cavalry. The disciplined Roman infantry opened ranks to allow Hannibal's elephants to pass through harmlessly, and after fierce fighting Scipio won the day. Hannibal survived to sue for terms, which included a 10,000-talent indemnity to be paid in 50 instalments and the loss of all Carthaginian lands outside North Africa. The city of Carthage survived, but its power was permanently crippled. Scipio celebrated the greatest triumph that Rome had yet witnessed, and in commemoration of his victory took the name Africanus.

The Second Punic War reaffirmed both the resilience of the Roman Republic and the remarkable loyalty it inspired from its Italian allies. Hannibal's genius may have been incomparable and his achievements the most memorable, but just as it had in the First Punic War Rome absorbed the punishment and ground out victory. That victory, however, came at a price. The massive manpower losses during the two wars inevitably impacted upon Rome's predominantly agricultural society. The population would recover with time, but the combination of social dislocation and the rising wealth acquired through Roman expansion played a crucial role in the internal crises Rome faced during the following century.

No less significant for the Republic was the emergence for the first time of a man whose personal authority and *gloria* threatened the collective rule of the Senate. When Scipio became consul in 205, before the Zama campaign, he had only just reached 30 years of age. He had never held any of the junior offices usually required before the consulship, and was given command ahead of older contemporaries like Fabius Maximus. Scipio's unprecedented career, encapsulated in his colossal triumph and the name Africanus, raised the bar of competition for all the senatorial elite. With the benefit of hindsight, we can recognize Scipio Africanus as the first of the Republican 'warlords', men whose charisma, wealth, and *gloria* gave them the status to rival the Senate. As yet the Republican principle of collective authority still held strong. But the competitive ethos of the Roman elite made it inevitable that others would seek to rival Scipio's achievements. The long line of warlords who emerged in the last two centuries of the Republic culminated in Julius Caesar and the emperor Augustus.

Carthago delenda est

Rome and Carthage would come into conflict one final time during the 2nd century, although the misnamed Third Punic War was a sad postscript to their long rivalry. After 202 Hannibal led a partial Carthaginian recovery, until he went into exile in 195 to avoid being handed over to Rome. Under the terms of its surrender, Carthage was forbidden to undertake any military action. This was exploited by neighbouring Numidia, who repeatedly seized Carthaginian territory. Every Carthaginian appeal to Rome was rejected. In 151 BC, the year after the last instalment of the indemnity was paid, Carthage lashed out against Numidia. In response, the Romans sent an embassy to investigate led by the hard-line senator Marcus Porcius Cato the Elder. Cato returned convinced of the threat that Carthage posed. From this time onwards, he concluded every speech that he made in the Senate with the famous words *Carthago delenda est* ('Carthage must be destroyed').

In 149 BC Rome once again despatched an army to Carthage. The Carthaginians submitted to every demand, giving up 300 hostages and surrendering all their weapons. The Romans then demanded that they abandon their homes and build a new city at least

10 miles from the sea. Driven to fight out of desperation, the Carthaginians resisted heroically for three years. Eventually, the Romans in frustration appointed as consul another rising champion too young to hold such an office, Publius Cornelius Scipio Aemilianus, the adopted grandson of Scipio Africanus. It was under his command that Carthage finally fell in 146. The city was destroyed, the surviving people enslaved, and the very ground cursed and sown with salt. Carthaginian North Africa was now a province of the Roman Republic.

Chapter 5
Mistress of the Mediterranean

Victory over Carthage made the Republic the leading power of the western Mediterranean. The First Punic War and its aftermath secured Roman rule over Sicily and Sardinia. The Second Punic War extended Roman influence into North Africa and Spain. A Roman province of Africa was only established in 146, but Sicily and Sardinia were governed by Rome from 241 and 237 respectively, and two provinces of Nearer Spain and Further Spain were created in 197. Beyond the borders of its provinces, the Republic exerted pressure through political, military, and economic superiority. There were still those in the west who resisted the dominion of Rome, and Roman armies continued to campaign against hostile Spanish tribes and later against the Celtic peoples of Gaul. But after Carthage's defeat, no western rival posed a direct threat to the Republic.

Rome enters the Hellenistic world

The traditional centres of power in the ancient Mediterranean, however, lay in the east. By 200 BC the glory days of the Greek city-states were lost in the past, but Greek language and culture remained the standard by which civilization was measured. Following the conquests of Alexander the Great, the eastern Mediterranean had been divided between an ever-shifting

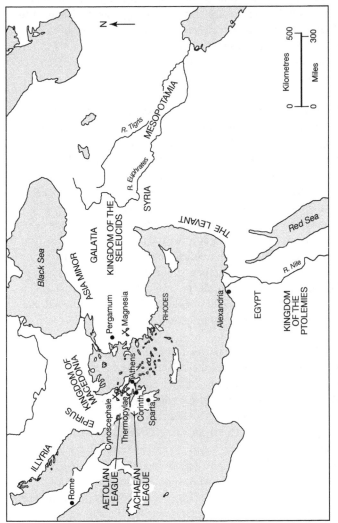

Map 6. Rome and the eastern Mediterranean

number of kingdoms, leagues, and cities. In the course of the 2nd century Rome came to dominate this complex Hellenistic world. Admiration for Greek culture brought new refinement to Rome even as Roman armies crushed those who sought to preserve Greek freedom, while Rome's eastern conquests brought new pressures to bear on the straining fabric of the Republic.

Alexander the Great died in 323 BC, leaving his vast conquests 'to the strongest'. His empire immediately shattered as his generals fought for control, and by the late 3rd century three major kingdoms had emerged: Macedon under the Antigonid dynasty, Syria under the Seleucids, and Ptolemaic Egypt. Greece itself was dominated by leagues of allied cities, notably the Aetolian League north of the Corinthian Gulf and the Achaean League in the Peloponnese. A few cities remained independent, including Sparta and Athens, but they were now of little political importance. Other states included the trading island of Rhodes and the kingdom of Pergamum in Asia Minor. As had been true throughout Greek history, the different states were part of a constantly changing web of wars and alliances, into which Rome came almost completely unprepared.

In military and political power, few of these states could in any way rival the Roman Republic. Nevertheless, for Rome, the Greek east had a higher significance. Greek culture had dominated the Mediterranean for centuries, and the Greeks were recognized as the arbiters of civilization. The Romans did not want simply to conquer the Greeks. They wanted the Greeks to accept them, not as barbarians (*barbaroi*) but as part of the civilized world. This desire for Greek respect had a profound effect on Roman involvement in Greek affairs. At the same time, the Republic remained an aggressive imperial power led by a highly ambitious senatorial elite. The resulting tensions played out in the long, and at times tragic, sequence of events that brought the eastern Mediterranean under Roman dominion.

The earliest direct contact between Rome and the Hellenistic cultures of the eastern Mediterranean had come with Pyrrhus' invasion of Italy in the early 3rd century. After this violent baptism, and faced by the more imminent threat of Carthage, Rome only slowly began to look towards the east. The initial Roman incursion across the Adriatic Sea took place in the years between the two great Punic Wars and was limited to the coastal region of Illyria. Even so, Rome attracted the attention of Philip V, king of Macedon. Determined to oppose Roman interference in his sphere of power, Philip signed a treaty of cooperation with Hannibal after Cannae. He did not act directly to aid Carthage, and the so-called First Macedonian War ended with a negotiated peace in 205 BC. But the Romans did not forget or forgive the king. Carthage was defeated in 202, and in 200 Rome declared war on Macedon.

It is important to step back for a moment and consider the significance of Rome's decision to open the Second Macedonian War. In 200 Rome and its allies were exhausted. The Second Punic War had barely concluded, the Battle of Zama was just two years in the past. Now the Republic deliberately provoked conflict with the homeland of Alexander. Why? Desire for revenge was certainly a factor, as was self-defence against possible Macedonian aggression. Rome also faced pressure to reassure its allies of its support, not only in Italy but in Greece, where a number of cities had appealed for Roman aid. The Roman desire for Greek acceptance must be remembered here, and so Rome demanded that Philip withdraw from Greece as the Greeks were under Roman protection. Yet despite all these motives, the Roman people did not want to fight. For almost the only time in Republican history, the *Comitia Centuriata* in 200 initially refused to endorse the consuls' request for a declaration of war. A second assembly was quickly summoned and persuaded to change its mind, but the hesitation revealed that it was a certain bloc within the elite, and above all the current magistrates, who actually wanted military action. Only through warfare could they emulate Scipio Africanus and attain the status and *gloria* that their competitive ethos demanded.

The Greeks welcomed the arrival of the Roman legions, and the Aetolian and Achaean Leagues rallied behind Rome. The war itself was not so straightforward. Macedon was a formidable kingdom, and the initial Roman armies had limited success. The solution, like the appointment of Scipio during the Second Punic War, was to elect the right man even if this meant ignoring Republican tradition. In 198 Titus Quinctius Flamininus was elected consul. He was a philhellene, a lover of Greek culture, and he spoke fluent Greek. Flamininus was therefore an ideal choice to win Greek support and promote Rome's civilized image. But he was just 30 years of age and had only previously been a quaestor. The career of Scipio had established a precedent to undermine the Republican system.

Flamininus was a cultured man, but he was a Roman noble. He wanted military *gloria*, and in 197 he finally defeated Philip at the Battle of Cynoscephale. In the military history of the ancient world, Cynoscephale confirmed the changing of the guard. The flexible legion formation developed by Scipio proved superior to the rigid Macedonian phalanx. Philip withdrew from Greece, and everyone held their breath awaiting Rome's decision. That decision came at the Isthmian Games of Corinth in 196. There, before the assembled representatives of the Greek states, Flamininus proclaimed the 'Freedom of Greece'.

> The Senate of Rome and Titus Quinctius Flamininus the proconsul, having defeated King Philip and the Macedonians in battle, leave the following states and cities free, without garrisons, subject to no tribute and in full enjoyment of their ancestral laws: the peoples of Corinth, Phocis, Locri, Euboea, Phthiotic Achaea, Magnesia, Thessaly and Perrhaebia.

According to Plutarch's *Life of Flamininus*, the shout of joy that rang out was so loud that ravens flying overhead fell to the ground dead. Greeks even honoured Flamininus as a god, the first Roman noble to receive such worship, and his cult still endured in Plutarch's time three centuries later.

'Freedom' has been a theme of propaganda throughout human history. The word had a particular resonance in the Greek world, where individual city-states had long fought for their autonomy, and the Hellenistic kings after Alexander had always paid at least lip service to that ideal. So too did Rome. What made Rome exceptional was that it acted on its promises. By 194, all Roman troops in the Greek east had been withdrawn. There would indeed be no garrisons, no tribute, and no new Roman provinces. In part, this was a matter of pragmatism. The Republic had neither the standing army nor the bureaucracy required to govern Greece directly. Yet Rome's restraint was also a measure of its admiration for the Greeks and their culture, an admiration Rome did not extend to its neighbours to the west. Throughout the 2nd century, Republican armies in Spain fought a series of wars for *gloria* and plunder. The wars were characterized by brutality, devastation, and treachery, and Spain has been aptly described as Rome's Vietnam. In the Greek east, by contrast, Rome initially relied more on diplomacy. Atrocities did happen, and Roman power was ruthless when threatened, but the Republic remained reluctant to impose direct rule. Rome had to appear 'civilized', and Greek opinion mattered.

Despite the withdrawal of the legions, the declaration of 196 BC confirmed that Rome now regarded the Greeks as under its protection. This was a direct challenge to the most prestigious of the Hellenistic kings, Antiochus III (the Great) of Seleucid Syria. Antiochus was an expansionist ruler who frightened Rome's allies Pergamum and Rhodes. In 195 BC he was joined by Hannibal following the latter's exile from Carthage, which further raised Roman concerns. Supported by the Aetolian League, who had grown disenchanted with Roman freedom, Antiochus marched into Greece in 191 BC.

Rome responded immediately. Antiochus was outflanked at Thermopylae, where the Spartans had resisted the Persians in 480 BC, and withdrew into Syria. He was pursued by the consul Lucius Cornelius Scipio, who had won election in part because his brother Scipio Africanus promised to serve alongside him. Antiochus outnumbered the Romans two to one, but his forces were vastly inferior in quality. Hannibal was wasted as a naval commander, and Antiochus was crushed at the Battle of Magnesia in 189 BC. The 15,000-talent indemnity that he had to pay dwarfed even that imposed upon Carthage after Zama, and revealed the sheer scale of wealth available to successful Roman commanders in the east. Rome then again withdrew its troops, but its dominion over Greece and Asia Minor had been confirmed. As for Hannibal, whom Antiochus was ordered to surrender, he remained elusive until 183 BC, when he was discovered by Flamininus in nearby Bithynia and took poison rather than submit to Rome.

Graecia capta

For the next two decades, the Republic continued the policy begun through the declaration of freedom at Corinth. No Roman troops were stationed in the Greek east, and no eastern territory was made a Roman province. The Greek influence upon Roman life, which had existed since Rome's first contact with the south Italian cities of Magna Graecia, now increased at a dramatic rate. Greek works of art flooded into Italy, knowledge of Greek language and literature attained a new importance for the Roman elite. Greek teachers, whether slaves or free, became a common feature of Roman noble households. A new hybrid Graeco-Roman culture began to emerge, encouraged in Rome by the philhellenes led by Flamininus and Scipio Africanus.

Not all Romans welcomed Greek influence with open arms. There were those who regarded philhellenism as a threat to the traditional virtues and virility of the Republic. Chief among such critics was Marcus Porcius Cato the Elder, who later in life would champion the destruction of Carthage. Cato himself was by no means ignorant of Greek culture (it was he who led the flanking attack at Thermopylae against Antiochus, repeating the Persian strategy of three centuries before). But he and his supporters regarded the Greeks as inferior, and feared that their influence would corrupt Roman values. In 155 an embassy of philosophers came to Rome from Athens. Carneades, a sceptic and the head of Plato's Academy, caused a scandal through his public lectures, in which he first argued in favour of justice and then on the next day refuted his own arguments. Cato caused the embassy to be sent home to prevent Carneades from misleading the Roman youth. It was a minor episode, but it symbolized the tensions within Rome, and the opposition of men like Cato to Flamininus and Scipio encouraged the more hard-line policy the Republic adopted towards the Greeks from the 170s onwards.

Rome may have respected Greek culture, but the Romans in their turn wanted the Greeks to recognize their authority. The Greek states were 'free' to rule themselves, just as Rome's Italian allies were. Like the allies, however, the Greeks were expected to stay quiet and to act only when commanded to do so. The Greeks had other ideas. The history of the Greek world was one of ever-changing rivalries and local conflicts, and this did not change with the coming of Rome. The Republican Senate found itself having to receive a constant stream of appeals requesting Roman arbitration of Greek disputes. Increasingly, the frustrated Romans simply supported whoever appealed to them first or whichever cause suited Rome's interests, regardless of the justice of a given case.

The chief victim of Rome's self-interest was Perseus of Macedon, the son and successor of Philip V. Perseus suffered repeatedly from biased senatorial decisions intended to keep Macedon in check. Those in the east who opposed Roman involvement in Greek affairs looked to Macedon for leadership, and in Roman eyes Perseus thus became a significant threat. In the absence of garrisons, tribute, or provincial government, Rome's influence over the Greeks depended on recognition of its power, and that recognition was being lost amidst rising anti-Roman feeling. The result was the Third Macedonian War, begun by Rome in 172 BC. Our two main sources, Polybius and Livy, reflect the effort that the Romans made to justify their aggression to the Greeks, but it is clear that Perseus did not wish to fight. In fact, Perseus won two minor skirmishes and then immediately offered to surrender and pay an indemnity in return for peace. Rome refused. Macedon had to be humbled permanently, and in 168 Perseus was defeated at the Battle of Pydna. The Macedonian monarchy was suppressed, and the region of Macedonia was divided into four weak republics that each paid tribute to Rome.

Even at this stage, Rome did not desire to seize land or create provinces in the east. What Rome did want was recognition of its power, and in the aftermath of the destruction of Macedon this was brutally enforced. 500 leading Aetolians were executed and 1,000 Achaeans were taken as hostages to Italy, one of whom was the future historian Polybius. Pyrrhus' former region of Epirus suffered still more, with 150,000 people enslaved, and Rome also reduced the power of Pergamum and Rhodes. Yet perhaps the most vivid statement of Rome's authority involved just a single man. While Roman attention was focused elsewhere, Antiochus IV of Syria invaded Ptolemaic Egypt. Near Alexandria, he was met by Roman envoys led by Gaius Popillius Laenas. When Antiochus received the Senate's command that he withdraw, the king requested time to consult with his advisors. Laenas 'drew a circle round the king with the rod he carried in his hand and said: "Before you move out of this circle, give me an answer to report to the Senate"' (Livy). Antiochus bowed to the will of Rome.

By 167 BC, no Greek state could doubt or challenge Roman power. Polybius wrote his *Histories* as a hostage in Rome and urged his fellow Greeks to accept Roman authority and avoid 'the fate that awaited those who opposed Rome'. His grim assessment was all too accurate. Following two decades of relative peace, the Macedonian republics revolted in 149 under a pretender to the throne named Andriscus. The revolt was destroyed, and Macedonia finally became a Roman province. Shortly afterwards, the Achaean League clashed with Sparta, and Rome decided that enough was enough. In 146, the same year that Carthage was destroyed, Corinth was razed to the ground at the orders of the Roman general Lucius Mummius. The devastation was recalled three centuries later by the Greek traveller Pausanias:

> At first, although the gates were open, Mummius hesitated to enter Corinth, suspecting that some ambush had been laid within the walls. But on the third day after the battle he proceeded to storm

6. Temple of Hercules Victor, Forum Boarium (Rome), dedicated by Lucius Mummius

Corinth and set it on fire. The majority of those found in it were put to the sword by the Romans, but the women and children Mummius sold into slavery. He also sold all the slaves who had been set free and had fought on the side of the Achaeans but had not fallen at once on the field of battle. The most admired votive offerings and works of art were carried off by Mummius.

It was an appropriate symbolic end to the 'freedom' granted to the Greeks in Corinth 50 years before. Greece was not officially made a province until the time of Augustus, and Syria and Egypt remained nominally independent. But the Roman Republic now held dominion over the legacy of the Greek city-states and Alexander the Great. The anger aroused by the decades of conflict and misunderstanding still simmered, and the tensions between Greeks and Romans never entirely faded away. In the longer term, however, the benefits for both cultures would far outweigh the costs. Roman rule ultimately brought peace, stability, and prosperity to the eastern Mediterranean, and in later centuries the Greek-speaking Byzantine Empire of Constantinople proudly proclaimed itself the heir of Rome. The Greeks for their part gave to Rome, not always willingly, their literature and art, and brought refinement and a new impetus to Roman life. In the words of the Augustan poet Horace, *Graecia capta ferum victorem cepit* ('captive Greece captured her savage conqueror').

Chapter 6
The cost of empire

The destruction of Carthage and Corinth in 146 BC reaffirmed the Roman Republic's dominance over the Mediterranean world. No enemy remained who could threaten the authority of the Senate or the military might of the legions. Little more than a century later, the Republic had collapsed. The political and social balance on which the Republic depended disintegrated into chaos and civil war, and ultimate power passed from the Senate and people of Rome to the solitary figure of an emperor.

In a very real sense, the Republic was the victim of its own success. The Republican constitution evolved to fulfil the needs of a small Italian city-state. As a political system it was a remarkable achievement, stable yet flexible and maintaining a careful balance between collective and individual rule. But that system was never intended to govern an empire. Expansion placed ever-increasing pressure on the Republic's political structures and on the collective authority of the senatorial elite. The same pressure fell no less strongly on Rome's social and economic structures. The early Romans had lived in a small agricultural world. An army of farmer-soldiers serving on seasonal campaigns struggled to meet the demands of the long wars with Carthage and of conflicts that spanned the length and breadth of the Mediterranean. The agrarian Roman economy could not help but be transformed by the flood of wealth and slaves that came with military victories. It was in the 2nd century that the full impact of these pressures came to bear upon Rome and Italy, setting in motion the chain of events that culminated in the 1st century in the fall of the Republic.

The seeds of crisis

The Second Punic War and the extension of Roman influence into the Greek east heralded a new generation within the Roman elite. The unprecedented career of Scipio Africanus challenged the fundamental Republican ethos of senatorial equality. For the first time, a Roman noble had emerged with the authority and popularity to oppose the collective will of the Senate. Nor would Scipio be the last. The competitive mentality of the Roman elite made it inevitable that other nobles would seek to equal or surpass Scipio. Flamininus defeated Philip of Macedon at the same young age as Scipio defeated Hannibal, and his triumph after the declaration of the 'Freedom of Greece' was nearly as magnificent. Scipio in turn reasserted his prestige by aiding his brother in the campaign against Antiochus of Syria. This escalating competition for wealth and *gloria* extended throughout the elite. In 188 BC a little-known noble, Gnaeus Manlius Vulso, exploited the war with Antiochus to launch an unprovoked plundering raid from Syria into the neighbouring region of Galatia. Vulso acted without senatorial approval, but was nevertheless awarded a triumph on his return to Rome. Such selfish actions would become a recurring feature of Roman foreign relations and highlighted the difficulty of controlling ambitious nobles, especially when they were far from Rome.

In the early 2nd century, the Senate's collective authority could still keep individual nobles in check. Even Scipio Africanus departed into voluntary exile after he was asked to provide financial accounts for the war with Antiochus, despite his protest that 'it was not proper for the Roman people to listen to anyone who accused Publius Cornelius Scipio, to whom his accusers owed it that they had the power of speech at all' (Livy). Efforts were made to prevent future nobles from emulating the careers of Scipio and Flamininus. In 180 BC the *Lex Villia Annalis* formalized the traditional structure of the *cursus honorum*, laying down the legal ages at which the different magistracies could be held. In c. 151 BC a subsequent law decreed that no individual could hold the consulship more than once. But the nobility's competitive ethos was too strong to be held in check by legal measures. Exceptional individuals continued to emerge to threaten the Senate's dominance, beginning with Scipio Aemilianus' illegal election as consul during the Third Punic War.

The expansion of Roman power, and the riches expansion brought, affected more than just the senatorial class. The 2nd century saw the appearance of the *equites* (equestrians or knights) as a separate bloc within Roman society. Originally, as the name suggests, the *equites* were the wealthier citizens who served in the cavalry when the Roman army was mustered. In the early Republic this included those of senatorial birth, and there was no clear division between senators and equestrians. Over time the influx of riches into Rome led to the emergence of a distinct social class, who possessed considerable wealth but lacked the status of the old senatorial families. Finally, in 129 BC, the senators were formally separated by law from the *ordo equester* (the equestrian order). Equestrians could not belong to the Senate unless they were elected to a magistracy and so passed into the senatorial order. Many were involved in industry and trade, areas traditionally barred to senators in theory if not always in practice, and equestrians were active in building projects and the collection of provincial taxes. The destruction of the great trading cities of Carthage and Corinth further assisted the rise of the equestrians, and they played a prominent part in Roman society and politics in the late Republic.

For the wider population of Rome and Italy, the economic consequences of expansion were even more far-reaching. Like all ancient societies the Roman Republic was characterized by a vast gulf between rich and poor, which only widened with the flood of wealth from the great wars of conquest. The rich became richer, for it was the nobility who received the greater proportion of the plunder. The poor suffered, as inflation brought rising prices and there was a sharp increase in the availability of slave labour. The numbers reveal the stark disparity. A Roman peasant could live on 240 sesterces per year. Yet a member of the equestrian order was expected to possess property valued at over 400,000 sesterces, and the traditional minimum wealth for a senator was 1,000,000 sesterces. Such mathematics may appear less exciting than the rise of the warlords, but the economic impact of expansion posed no less of a threat to the unity and stability of the Republic.

In a world where agriculture was the chief basis of wealth, the rich devoted their new-found resources to their estates. Slaves provided the labour for larger fields (*latifundia*, 'wide lands') and aided the cultivation of grapes and olives for the commercial production of wine and olive oil. So high were slave numbers, with 150,000 taken from Epirus alone in 167 BC, that slave revolts became a serious danger as Spartacus would demonstrate in the early 1st century. No less significantly, this growth of noble estates and slave labour, combined with a gradual rise in population numbers, placed pressure on the Roman and Italian small farmers who provided the backbone of the Republican army. Those unable to hold land of their own drifted to the towns and to Rome, where they swelled the volatile Roman urban mob. And as those without land could not meet the property requirement needed to qualify for the *assidui* (those eligible for military service), they could not now serve in the army.

The exact scale of the social crisis that the Republic faced in the 2nd century is difficult to judge from the limited evidence. Certainly not all small farmers disappeared, and when Rome really needed to rally sizeable armies, as in 146 BC, it was able to do so. Nevertheless, army recruitment did become a problem. The ongoing wars in Spain were particularly unpopular, and in 151 and

137 BC there was such opposition to the military levy that the consuls were thrown in prison by the tribunes of the plebs. The Italian allies, whose manpower and loyalty were so crucial to Rome's success, were also unhappy. They were asked to provide troops for longer and more distant wars, and while they received their share of the plunder they were still denied any political voice. The emergence of the equestrians desiring a greater role in public affairs and the volatility of the urban mob added to the discontent. All that was required was a spark to ignite the tensions. In 133 BC that spark was lit with the election as tribune of the plebs of Tiberius Sempronius Gracchus.

The Gracchi

Tiberius Gracchus (born c. 163 BC) came from the Republic's highest nobility. His father of the same name twice held the consulship and his mother was Cornelia, the daughter of Scipio Africanus. The young Tiberius thus faced enormous pressure to achieve the success expected of him. The conventional path to *gloria* was through military success and the consulship. But Tiberius instead made a conscious choice to pursue social reform through the office of tribune. According to his younger brother Gaius, Tiberius once passed through northern Italy en route to Spain. As he travelled:

> He saw for himself how the country had been deserted by its native inhabitants and how those who tilled the soil or tended the flocks were barbarian slaves.

Tiberius' solution was simple but inspired. Upon his election as tribune in 133 BC, he proposed that land should be given to unemployed small farmers, thereby in one stroke easing social tensions, reducing the urban mob, and improving army recruitment. To achieve this, he wished to redistribute the *ager publicus*, state-owned land taken during Rome's earlier conquests in Italy and rented out by the state to the nobility. Legally, no Roman could own more

7. Cornelia and the Gracchi (1861)

than 500 *iugera* (312.5 acres) of public land, although this limit had
long been ignored. Tiberius intended to confiscate all land held in
excess of the limit, and divide that land among the unemployed
smallholders in blocks of 30 *iugera* (20 acres). These blocks would be
inalienable, and so the rich could not buy the land back.

Any proposal to tamper with land ownership in a conservative agricultural society aroused intense fear. Much public land had been held by families for generations and had been inherited, sold, and even used for family tombs. Above all, Tiberius was opposed by the senatorial nobility, who had the most to lose. Unable to convince the Senate to support his bill, Tiberius invoked the legislative power of the tribune and turned to the *Concilium Plebis*, the popular assembly. This was not illegal, but proposed laws were traditionally agreed in advance by the Senate. Moreover, Tiberius' fellow tribunes were again nobles, and in the assembly they continued to resist him. One, Marcus Octavius, imposed his tribune's veto. In response, Tiberius declared that a tribune must serve the people: 'If he annuls the powers of the people, he ceases to be a tribune at all.' Octavius was deposed and dragged from the assembly, an action without precedent in a system based on precedent, and Tiberius' *Lex Sempronia agraria* became law.

The new law could not be enforced. Land markings were blurred, records were poor, and Tiberius found himself constantly blocked. Desperate, he turned to an unexpected source for aid. In mid-133 BC, King Attalus III of Pergamum died without heirs and left his kingdom to Rome. Tiberius seized Attalus' treasury to fund his land redistribution, and decreed that the people would decide the organization of the new province of Asia. By doing so, Tiberius challenged the whole order of Roman government, for finance and foreign affairs had always remained in the hands of the Senate. Rumours spread that Tiberius desired personal power, even that he aspired to the hated status of king. Then he sought re-election as tribune to continue his reforms. This was the final straw, a rejection of the Republican principle of annual magistracies. Rioting broke out as he presented himself for re-election. Over 300 were killed, and Tiberius was struck down by a senatorial mob, his body thrown into the Tiber.

With Tiberius' death, his agrarian reform programme collapsed. Only to be revived in 123 BC, when Tiberius' younger brother

Gaius (born 154 BC) followed his lead and won election as tribune. No one could question Gaius' courage, for his brother's fate lay before him and still he chose the path of reform. Like Tiberius, he sought the redistribution of land to aid the small farmers, but Gaius' proposals were much broader and impacted on all levels of Republican society. To support the growing urban poor of Rome, he set a fixed price at which the state would sell grain. There was little organized welfare or charity in Republican Rome, and the importance of keeping the people happy with food and entertainment was immortalized by the later satirist Juvenal as the 'bread and circuses' of the Roman Empire. Gaius also aided the newly emerging equestrian order. He organized the tax farming of the Roman provinces, through which equestrian companies paid an agreed sum to the state and then oversaw tax collection, keeping any profit made. At the same time, he gave the equestrians control over the criminal courts that previously had been in the hands of senatorial juries. This prevented senatorial abuse of the courts, but opened the provinces to the equestrians who could and did prosecute honest senatorial governors who tried to check their exploitation.

Gaius' wide-ranging programme secured him enormous prestige, to the extent that, unlike Tiberius, he was able to stand successfully for re-election as tribune in 122 BC. And even more than Tiberius, he aroused the hatred of the Senate. Gaius' appeal to the urban populace and the equestrian order threatened senatorial authority, and his personal standing once again led to accusations of excessive ambition. Gradually, the Senate chipped away at Gaius' popularity. Other noble tribunes were used to counter or outbid his policies, forcing Gaius to seek new supporters. He therefore proposed a law that would grant full Roman citizenship to the Italian allies. Such a law would have eased the tensions rising in Italy, but was opposed both by the nobility and by the Roman plebs, who feared competition for food and jobs. Gaius' failure further weakened his position, and his appearance in armour at the elections for 121 BC triggered another massive riot. The Senate passed the first ever *senatus consultum ultimum* (the final decree of the Senate), giving the consuls authority to take whatever action was necessary to defend the Republic. 3,000 of Gaius' supporters were killed, and Gaius himself committed suicide. Whoever brought Gaius' head was promised its weight in gold, and the man who did so first removed the brain and poured in molten lead before claiming the reward.

Later generations remembered the Gracchi as champions of the Roman people, and their statues received worship like the shrines of the gods. But the problems that Tiberius and Gaius had sought to resolve still remained, and their controversial careers undermined the stability of senatorial government. The Gracchi thus marked the beginning of the chaotic century that led to the Republic's collapse. As tensions over landholding, army recruitment, and allied rights continued to simmer, a series of military crises opened the way for the next generation of warlords to challenge the Senate's collective authority.

The rise of the warlords

The first crisis to break out was the Jugurthine War (112–105 BC). Jugurtha was the king of Numidia, on the border of the Roman province of Africa. In 112 he ordered a massacre of the Roman and Italian traders in the region, an insult to which the Republic had to respond. Militarily, Jugurtha posed little danger to Rome. But his exploitation of Roman corruption was legendary, celebrated in his notorious remark that Rome 'is a city up for sale, and its days are numbered should it find a buyer'. The incompetence and greed of the senatorial generals sent against him allowed the war to drag on, until in 107 Gaius Marius was elected consul and took over command. Marius was a *novus homo*, the first of his family to reach the consulship. He owed his election to his reputation as an experienced soldier, while he had also married a Julia, the aunt of Julius Caesar, from the ancient if politically insignificant Julian clan. Jugurtha's forces were swiftly defeated, although the war

8. Silver denarius depicting the capture of Jugurtha (minted 56 BC)
Obverse: Head of Diana
Reverse: Sulla seated on a raised chair while King Bocchus of Numidia kneels
before him offering an olive-branch and Jugurtha kneels behind Sulla's chair with
his hands tied behind his back

only ended in 105 with the king's capture by Marius' subordinate
and rival Lucius Cornelius Sulla.

While the war in Africa slowly drew to a close, a far more real
threat to Rome emerged from the north. In the late 2nd century
massed German tribes moved into Gaul and northern Italy.
Reportedly over 300,000 strong, these were not raiding warriors
but entire migrating peoples, the first of many waves of Germanic
tribes that moved into Roman territory due to pressures further
east. The Cimbri and Teutones inflicted a series of crushing
defeats upon Roman armies, culminating at Orange in 105 BC
where 80,000 Roman soldiers died, a defeat even worse than
Cannae a century before. In this state of emergency, Marius
returned from Africa and celebrated his triumph over Jugurtha.
Hailed as Rome's saviour, he was elected consul every year from
104 to 100 by popular demand. Five successive consulships made
a mockery of the annual Republican magistracies, but Marius
justified the people's faith by destroying the German tribes in two
great victories at Aix-en-Provence in 102 and Vercellae in 101. The
gloria from his successes and his domination of the consulship

gave Marius unprecedented status, and once again raised the stakes of Roman noble competition.

Marius was the first of the great warlords who dominated the last century of the Republic. In the long term, however, no less important than his career was Marius' reorganization of the Republican army. During his campaigns in Africa and against the Germans, Marius accepted as recruits anyone prepared to volunteer, not only the *assidui* who met the traditional property requirement but those without land, the *capite censi* or 'head count'. In consequence, Rome for the first time acquired a truly uniform professional army. As Marius' new soldiers had no land to farm, they could serve for extended periods with rigorous training and discipline. As they were poor, they were all equipped alike by the state. The men were known as 'Marian mules', marching in heavy legionary armour and carrying a 25-kilogram pack as well as two *pila* and the Spanish *gladius*. One of the two spears had a head weakly secured by nails, an invention of Marius which meant that when the spear hit a target the head bent and the spear could not be thrown back. Marius likewise revised army formation. The 120-man maniple of Scipio Africanus had been ideally suited to defeat the elephants at Zama and the more rigid Macedonian phalanx. Now the smaller maniple was replaced as the basic army unit by the 600-man cohort, a denser body of men better able to resist massed Germanic charges. From these reforms emerged the famed legions of the Roman Empire.

The Marian reforms forged a tough professional infantry army. They also marked the abandonment of the old ideal of a Roman citizen militia. Marius' landless volunteers were promised a farm at the end of their service as an inducement to recruits. Responsibility for fulfilling that promise lay with the general to whom the new soldiers took their oath of loyalty. Thus the armies became personal, loyal to their general not to the Senate or the Roman state. Earlier in the 2nd century, the Senate had managed to keep a check on great individuals like Scipio Africanus and preserve collective leadership of the Republic. Now the social and economic pressures that the Gracchi had been unable to resolve led to the emergence of private armies in the service of men driven to compete for status and *gloria*. The man who exploited the new possibilities was not Marius, who was more soldier than politician. It was Marius' rival Lucius Cornelius Sulla, and another of the unresolved tensions of the 2nd century provided just the opportunity that he desired.

Throughout the crises of the previous three decades, the status of Rome's Italian allies had remained a point of contention. Many of Marius' recruits were Italians rather than Roman citizens, and by 100 BC Italians made up two-thirds of the army. Yet they still had no political rights in Rome. Italian demands for a share in Roman citizenship steadily grew more strident, until in 91 BC the murder of their champion, the tribune Marcus Livius Drusus, sparked the Social War (*socii*, 'allies'). Confronted by a numerous enemy trained and equipped on Roman principles, Rome initially struggled. Fortunately for the Romans, the aim of the vast majority of the allies was not to destroy Rome but to force concessions. In 88 Rome finally acknowledged the allied demands and conflict immediately subsided. With hindsight, the Italians' hard-won victory in their struggle for Roman citizenship was a crucial stage in the creation of a lasting empire. Over the following centuries the rights granted to the Italians were gradually extended to all Rome's subject peoples, uniting the Mediterranean under the umbrella of Roman identity.

In the course of the Social War, Sulla supplanted Marius as Rome's premier general through a series of victories in southern Italy. At the war's end he was elected consul, just as Rome received warning of a new enemy, King Mithridates of Pontus on the Black Sea. Sulla was given command of the army gathered to drive back Mithridates' invasion of the Roman province of Asia. What happened next was a grim omen for the future of the Republic. Before Sulla could leave for the east, a radical tribune named

Sulpicius Rufus passed a law that transferred the command from Sulla to Marius. Like Caesar 40 years later on the banks of the Rubicon, Sulla faced the choice between political oblivion and civil war. And like Caesar, Sulla would not back down. For the first time in Republican history, a Roman army advanced upon Rome.

Sulla's march on Rome was the natural consequence of Roman noble ambition and the Marian reforms. In his desire for *gloria* and pre-eminence, Sulla appealed to his soldiers to fight to defend his *dignitas*. Those soldiers were loyal to him, not to the state, and depended upon him for the land grants that they had been promised. The Senate's collective authority, already weakened by the pressures of expansion and the challenge of the Gracchi, had no power over the warlord with his private army. The Republic's fate now lay in the hands of individual generals whose competitive ethos and striving for supremacy could not be restrained. The disintegration of the Republic had begun.

Chapter 7
Word and image

The rise and fall of the Roman Republic is an extraordinary tale. Yet the metamorphosis of Rome from a small city-state to the mistress of an empire was not simply a story of military conquests and political crises. Literature and art bring to life the world of the ancient Romans, looking beyond the marching legions and senatorial debates. The voices of Republican authors have echoed down to modern times, from the early playwrights Plautus and Terence to the great generation of Catullus, Cicero, and Caesar. The quality of Republican art has not always received the admiration it deserves, but is visible in superb statue busts and in many of the finest paintings preserved in the buried town of Pompeii. These achievements merit attention in their own right, and laid the foundations for the golden age of Roman culture under the first emperor Augustus.

In culture no less than in political and military history, the earliest years of Rome are hidden behind the veil of the past. There is no trace of Roman literary activity from before the 3rd century, and while artistic accomplishment certainly existed all too little has survived the passage of time. What can be said with confidence is that Roman culture, like every other aspect of Roman life, drew from the very beginning on the traditions of the neighbouring peoples. The Etruscans to the north and the Greeks to the south were early influences, and Greece's cultural impact upon Rome inevitably grew with increasing involvement in the Greek-speaking east. Nevertheless, Rome's culture remained its own. Here, as elsewhere, we recognize the particular Roman genius to absorb and assimilate the qualities of others and transform those models into something new and uniquely Roman.

The first flowering of Latin literature

The origins of Latin literature bear witness to that genius for assimilation and transformation. From what little evidence we possess, down to the 3rd century writing was used in Rome for record-keeping and for legal and religious formulae. Literacy was limited to the elite, and public entertainment was provided through games and local dramatic performances. It was from the Greek cities of southern Italy that literature arrived in Rome, and the large-scale adaptation of classical Greek works and genres into Latin forms began. The earliest Latin poet whom we know by name was himself a Greek from Tarentum, Livius Andronicus (c. 280–200). Brought to Rome as a slave, Andronicus was later freed and made a living as a teacher and playwright. Only a few fragments of his works survive, but it is not difficult to identify his chief source of inspiration. Andronicus' Latin translation of Homer's *Odyssey* was used in Roman schools for centuries, and his tragic plays likewise drew heavily on the stories and heroes of the Trojan War.

In the next generation, this dependence upon Greek inspiration and models found a new expression through the rise of Roman comedy. The early Latin writers from whom the greatest volume of material has been preserved were two comic playwrights, Titus Maccius Plautus (c. 254–184) and Publius Terentius Afer (c. 195–159). Neither was born in Rome, for Plautus came from Umbria and Terence was a slave born in North Africa, but both had a lasting impact on Roman culture. Some 21 plays of Plautus survive more or less complete (a little under half of his original output), together with all 6 of the known plays of Terence. Their works were performed at state games and during the funerary celebrations of leading families, and they provide a goldmine of information about Republican society and values. Yet their plays were once again adapted from Greek originals. We get a sense of how that adaptation was achieved from the prologue of one of Plautus' best-known plays, the *Miles Gloriosus* (the Swaggering Soldier):

> Now you're all settled, I'll tell you about the plot
> And explain the title of the play you're about to see
> On this happy and festal occasion.
> In the Greek this play is entitled *Alazon – The Braggart*;
> Which in Latin we have translated by *Gloriosus*.
> This town is Ephesus. The soldier you saw just now
> Going off to the forum – he's my lord and master;
> He is also a dirty liar, a boastful, arrogant,
> Despicable perjurer and adulterer.

Plautus' play was based upon a (lost) Greek original and was set in the Greek-speaking city of Ephesus in Asia Minor. The title character of the arrogant mercenary soldier was more Greek than Roman, as is his name Pyrgopolynices (roughly 'mighty conqueror of fortresses'). Yet the star of the play is Palaestrio, the slave who delivers the prologue and masterminds the soldier's downfall. The clever slave is a recurring Plautine character who figures more prominently in his works than in their Greek originals and clearly appealed to Plautus' Roman audience. Plautus' choice of moral emphasis similarly suits his Roman context, set alongside the vulgarity and slapstick that also characterize his plays. The result is a hybrid Roman–Greek form of drama whose influence can be traced far beyond its Republican roots, from Shakespeare's *The Comedy of Errors* to *A Funny Thing Happened on the Way to the Forum*.

Roman historiography no less than drama traced its origins to the Greeks, who had coined the term *historia* ('inquiry'). Quintus

Fabius Pictor, a senator who fought in the Second Punic War, became the first Roman to write an historical account of Rome around the year 200 BC. Strikingly, he wrote not in Latin but in Greek. A number of Greek histories of Rome had already been composed by this time, and it was these Greek historians who originally traced Roman descent back to the Trojan War and the travels of Aeneas and other Homeric heroes. Romans like Fabius Pictor embraced and developed such stories. Pictor's work is now lost, but he drew upon Rome's association with Aeneas and intertwined with that legend the local Italian fables that became the foundation myth of Romulus and Remus. From this fusion of Greek and Italian traditions emerged the Roman perception of their origins and historical identity. Fabius Pictor set out Rome's story in Greek terms incorporated into a Greek vision of antiquity, but his values remained Roman and he affirmed Rome's special place in the wider Mediterranean world.

Before Fabius Pictor, the only Republican historical sources were the family records of the great noble houses, which were somewhat prone to self-glorification, and the record of magistracies and major events kept by the priestly college of *pontifices*. Finally, in the early 2nd century, Latin historical writing began. Quintus Ennius (c. 239–c. 169) was not a prose historian but a poet, and his *Annales* was an historical epic that told Rome's history from the fall of Troy to his own time. Near the beginning of the poem Ennius hailed himself as the reincarnation of Homer, who had appeared to him in a dream, and like Fabius Pictor he combined Homeric legends with Roman traditions. The *Annales* was the national epic of Rome until supplanted by Virgil's *Aeneid*. Sadly, however, Ennius' text is again largely lost, and is remembered today through passages quoted by other authors. Perhaps the most famous, and very apt from a man who lived through the Second Punic War, being *Qui vincit non est victor nisi victus fatetur* ('The victor is not victorious if the vanquished does not consider himself so').

The last great name of the early years of Latin literature is the familiar one of Marcus Porcius Cato the Elder (234–149). The conservative Cato was famed for his hostility towards Greek culture, and it was appropriate that he wrote the first Latin prose history of Rome. His now fragmentary work, begun after 170, was entitled *Origines*. Determined to uphold Republican ideals, Cato emphasized service to the state as greater than the individual and preferred to identify military commanders by their rank rather than their name. Yet this did not prevent him from glorifying his own achievements, and despite Cato's aversion to Hellenism he too traced Roman descent back to Aeneas and the Trojan War.

Cato was not alone in his devotion to preserving Roman traditions and virtues. Knowledge of Greek language and literature was expected of the Roman nobility by the 2nd century, but so too was adherence to the values of the Republic. This determination found literary expression in the one genre that the Romans claimed as their own without Greek inspiration: satire. Combining scathing social and political criticism with literary parody and moral judgement, satire offered a contemporary commentary on the Republic's rapidly changing world. The first true Roman satirist was Gaius Lucilius (d. 102 BC), a friend of Scipio Aemilianus who had gathered around himself a literary circle. Only fragments of Lucilius' verse satires survive, but the genre he established endured. Lucilius offered a model for the Augustan poet Horace and for Juvenal, perhaps the finest of the Roman satirists, whose works gave us the sayings 'bread and circuses' and 'who guards the guards themselves?'.

Catullus and Cicero

The cultural history of Rome under the Republic reached its zenith in the 1st century. Even as the Republican system itself collapsed into civil war, writers of genius raised Latin literature to new heights. The lyric poetry of Gaius Valerius Catullus (c. 84–54 BC) combined subtle Greek allusions with everyday Latin expressions to achieve a power that would stand out in any age. Catullus drew on the refined Hellenistic poetry of Alexandria, and on the greatest female poet of antiquity, Sappho of Lesbos. He could describe sexuality in the crudest possible terms, yet his insight into the psychology of love was profound and earned from hard experience. To quote in full one of his shortest but most compelling poems:

Odi et amo: quare id faciam, fortasse requiris,
Nescio, sed fieri sentio et excrucior

I hate and I love. And if you ask me how,
I do not know: I only feel it, and I am torn in two.

(Poem 85)

Catullus' prime source of torture and inspiration was the woman he named 'Lesbia', a pseudonym derived from Sappho which probably concealed the identity of Clodia Metelli, the wife of Quintus Metellus Celer. Clodia is known from a damning speech by Cicero, and among other dubious activities she was accused of poisoning her husband and of incest with her brother (and Cicero's great enemy) Publius Clodius. For Catullus, 'Lesbia' was a figure of lust, love, and pain. He envied the pet sparrow she played with and mourned its death (Poems 2–3), counting as numerous as grains of sand or stars in the sky the number of her kisses needed to satisfy his desire (Poem 7). But he denounced her infidelity ('live with your three hundred lovers, open your legs to them all at once': Poem 11) and prayed for release:

I do not now expect – or want – my love returned,
Nor cry to the moon for Lesbia to be chaste:
Only that the gods cure me of this disease
And, as I once was whole, make me now whole again.

(Poem 76)

The themes of Catullus' poetry strike at the heart of the human condition, hence their appeal. His works refer only in passing to the conflicts of the Republic's closing years, and illuminate the living social world of Rome that political narratives tend to conceal. Our other principal guide into that world was far more politically minded than Catullus, but his voluminous writings are of even greater value in bringing Rome alive: Marcus Tullius Cicero (106–43 BC).

We know more of the life and character of Cicero than of any other man or woman in the long history of ancient Rome. He is at the same time our single most valuable source for the last age of the Republic and a leading participant in the dramatic events of those years. Above all, to a greater degree than any of his contemporaries like Pompeius Magnus or Julius Caesar, Cicero through his writings comes down to us as a human being. He was a flawed and inconsistent man, but idealistic, principled, and at times courageous, and he gave his life in the doomed defence of the failing Republic.

Cicero ('chickpea') was born in Gaius Marius' home town of Arpinum, southwest of Rome, and like Marius he was a *novus homo*. Unlike Marius, and very unusually for a Roman 'new man', he was never a good soldier. What brought Cicero to prominence was his gift as an orator. Public speaking was an essential skill before the rise of modern mass media, and Cicero was the greatest orator Rome ever produced. Near the end of his life, he delivered one speech so powerful that Julius Caesar, himself Rome's second greatest orator, dropped the papers he was carrying in shock. More than 50 of Cicero's speeches survive, preserving his talent and providing a priceless glimpse into the murky depths of Republican law, society, and politics.

In 70 BC Cicero burst onto the Roman political scene with the prosecution of Gaius Verres, the corrupt senatorial governor of Sicily who had exploited his post to loot the province. Verres' defence team was led by Quintus Hortensius Hortalus, the leading trial orator of the time. But Cicero's opening speech and the flood of witnesses and evidence that he presented were so damning that Hortensius simply quit and Verres went into voluntary exile.

The trial of Verres saw Cicero first lay down the political manifesto that he upheld throughout his career. Essentially a conservative, he believed in the collective leadership of the Senate and the traditional structures of the Republic. However, he was also an idealist, who so admired the traditional Republican system that he ignored its flaws. Verres' abuses reflected the corruption that grew within the Roman elite as the government structure struggled to cope with the demands of ruling the Mediterranean. Cicero described his vision of Rome in the *De Re Publica* (completed in 51 BC), a now fragmentary treatise modelled on Plato's *Republic*. A Senate that ruled with clear moral authority guided a quiet, passive populace and channelled the ambitions of the individual nobility. Cicero simply assumed that such a system would ensure peace, and he offered no solution to the socio-economic problems of the 2nd century, the urban mob, or the private armies of warlords like Marius and Sulla. His state was an ideal, not a reality.

Yet Cicero cannot be dismissed as merely a philosophical dreamer. He was a leading figure in the transmission of Greek philosophical ideas into Latin, but like Plautus and Catullus in their fields he adapted his Greek models to serve Roman ends. In particular, Cicero sought far more strongly than Plato to make his dream a reality. Like most of his contemporaries, Cicero saw ethical and political philosophy as utterly inseparable. Political decline was understood as a consequence of moral decline, and so in turn political reform required moral reform. Cicero therefore offered practical advice on how one should live in a troubled world. In one of his last works, the treatise *On Duties* (44–43 BC), Cicero turned to the morality of the Roman past to provide guidance on correct behaviour in the present. The greatest good is service to the state, and the greatest service to the state is to oppose a tyrant. Written in the immediate aftermath of Caesar's murder, there is a very real contemporary force behind Cicero's insistence that it is not only necessary but morally right to kill those who seek autocratic power.

Cicero's speeches and treatises reveal his vision of the Republic and his conception of a proper moral Roman life. They do not reveal the man himself. For this, we must read the richest treasure that Cicero bequeathed to posterity, his letters. Over 800 letters survive, spanning the last 25 years of his life. Many are to Cicero's confidant and closest friend, Titus Pomponius 'Atticus' (so named as he loved Athens and often lived there). It was Atticus who helped organize the publication of the letters after Cicero's death, although he first removed his own replies. Through the letters we see Cicero respond to events as they occur without the benefit of hindsight or later editing, from his shifting relationships with Pompeius and Caesar to his savage glee at Caesar's death and the end of his dictatorship ('How I should like you to have invited me to that most gorgeous banquet on the Ides of March').

In his letters, the orator and philosopher is revealed with all his failings. He is weak, indecisive, vain, vindictive, and often mistaken in his judgement of himself and others. But he is also intelligent, caring, idealistic, and on occasion heroic. He tried to live according to his ideals, even though at times he knew that he failed, and ultimately he gave his life in defence of those ideals. Cicero died a year and a half after Caesar, killed at the orders of the Second Triumvirate led by Marcus Antonius and Gaius Julius Caesar Octavianus (the future Emperor Augustus). Yet it was Augustus who provided Cicero's fitting epitaph. Seeing his grandson reading one of Cicero's works, he picked up the book to study and then returned it: 'A learned man, my child, a learned man and a lover of his country.'

Brick and marble

Across the span of over 2,000 years that separates us from the Roman Republic, the writings of Plautus, Catullus, and Cicero provide our most accessible window into the Roman world. The evidence of material culture, of art and architecture, is more fragmentary and difficult to interpret for the non-specialist. Yet it is an essential part of Rome's cultural achievement and no less essential for our understanding of the physical environment in which Roman men and women went about their lives. Much has been lost to the passage of time or lies concealed beneath the later monuments of the Roman Empire. But what has survived from the Republic includes works of both utility and great beauty. Like every other aspect of Roman culture, Republican art and architecture drew on numerous outside influences and yet remained distinctively Roman.

Few physical traces of early Rome have been preserved. The bronze Capitoline Wolf (Figure 1) is probably of Etruscan craftsmanship, although the accompanying infants were added under Pope Sixtus IV (1471–84), and the Etruscan influence on Roman material culture was extensive. Roman house and temple design built upon Etruscan models, while the Etruscans were likewise known for decorated pottery and for statues and sarcophagi made from local terracotta (early Italy had no accessible source of marble). The Etruscans in turn drew inspiration from the Greeks, and the increasing impact of Greek culture on the Republic is visible in art no less than in literature. The adaptation of these external influences to serve Rome's changing needs drove some of the finest work of the Republican age.

The Romans themselves regarded their architectural prowess as one of their greatest contributions to ancient civilization. In part, that contribution was highly functional. The Greek Dionysius of Halicarnassus was moved to write that the three most magnificent achievements of Rome were 'the aqueducts, the paved roads, and the construction of the sewers'. Such constructions were hardly Roman inventions, but they were raised by the Romans to new heights of design and efficiency. Existing architectural elements were used on a new scale, particularly arches and vaults, and the

Romans made extensive use of concrete, which was more readily available in Italy than quality cut stone and did not require skilled labour.

Only a tiny fraction of the architectural works of the Republic can be reconstructed today. The houses of everyday people leave little physical trace, and the surviving monuments of ancient Rome primarily glorify Augustus and the later emperors. Nevertheless, we can gain a glimpse of the setting in which Republican history unfolded. The urban focus of Rome remained the Forum at the foot of the Capitoline Hill, where the Senate met and magistrates performed their civic duties. In the area around the Forum and along the triumphal *Via Sacra*, monuments commemorated Roman achievements and the heroes of previous generations. The glories of the past pervaded Republican social and political life, reinforcing the pressure on those in the present to emulate and surpass their ancestors.

9. **The Forum Romanum**

It is a reflection of Roman piety as well as Roman noble competition that the most characteristic public architectural form under the Republic was the temple. Roman temples followed an Etruscan-Italian model that differed significantly from the temples of ancient Greece. The most famous temple of Rome, that of Jupiter on the Capitoline Hill, can now be reconstructed only from the outline of its ground plan. The temple stood on a high podium and had to be approached up a flight of steps at the front, unlike most Greek temples which were built on a lower base and could be approached from any direction. It was here that the celebration of a triumph culminated, as the returning general offered sacrifice to Jupiter for his victory.

The temples of Rome proliferated with its expansion and the accompanying wealth. For the nobility, construction of a temple was an ideal way to commemorate their success publicly while at the same time thanking the gods for their favour. According to legend, the original temple of Castor and Pollux in the Roman Forum was built to honour the aid that the divine twins had given to Rome at the Battle of Lake Regillus in the early 5th century. A few columns survive from a later rebuilding of that temple under the emperor Tiberius. Further temples were dedicated by nobles from the proceeds of war. In the mid-2nd century, the round temple was built that still stands in the Forum Boarium (Figure 6). The exact identity of this temple and its deity is debated, but most probably this was the temple of Hercules Victor, and the most likely dedicator was Lucius Mummius, who destroyed Corinth in 146 BC. If true, there is a certain irony that his temple is the oldest extant marble building in Rome and the first known Roman temple to include columns of the Corinthian order.

Temples were not the only monuments through which the Roman nobility celebrated their accomplishments. The triumphal arch was a Republican creation, although all surviving honorific arches in Rome belong to the imperial period. Scipio Africanus erected the most prominent Republican arch, on the road that led up the

Capitoline Hill. More unusual monuments appeared in the 1st century as the intensity of noble competition grew ever stronger. The Theatre of Pompey, begun by Pompeius Magnus in 55 BC, was Rome's first permanent theatre in contrast to the temporary wooden structures previously in use. This theatre building was only one part of a much larger complex, which also included numerous images celebrating Pompeius' deeds and a temple to his personal patron deity, Venus Victrix. Here, beneath the statue of his rival, Julius Caesar would be murdered in 44 BC.

Caesar's own monument was on an even grander scale. Beside the sprawling Forum Romanum he began the Forum of Julius Caesar, with a temple at one end to Venus Genetrix, Venus the ancestress of the Julian family. Rome's rising population and the demands of governing an empire made an additional forum a practical necessity, but in scope and ambition Caesar's Forum prefigured the imperial age. Unfinished at the time of Caesar's murder, the Forum was completed by his adopted son Augustus, who would go on to dedicate his own Forum and to declare without much exaggeration that 'I found Rome built of bricks, I leave her clothed in marble'.

Painting and sculpture

The interaction of external influences and noble competition drove the evolution of Roman art no less than architecture. Painting is a fragile medium, yet has survived from Republican Rome on a surprising scale. A few damaged examples come from Rome itself, including the earliest extant Roman wall painting, the so-called Esquiline Historical Fragment (Figure 2). Approximately dated to the 3rd century BC, the Fragment celebrates a victory over the Samnites won by a Roman general from the Fabian family, in whose tomb the triumphal scene was depicted. But the greatest treasures of Republican painting we owe to the tragedy that befell Pompeii and Herculaneum with the eruption of Mount Vesuvius in AD 79. As the tragedy occurred over a century after the Republic's fall, it is easily forgotten that much of the art preserved by the ash and pumice that buried Pompeii dates to Republican times. It is primarily from the evidence of Pompeii that we can reconstruct the evolution of Roman painting in the 2nd and 1st centuries BC.

The First or 'Masonry' Style of Roman painting was a product of Rome's growing wealth and the universal human desire of the less well-off to copy those more fortunate. During the 2nd century, luxurious villas with rich marble fittings appeared in Italy. Those who could not afford expensive marble turned instead to painted plaster. Rectangular panels were decorated to imitate coloured stone. More impressive to modern eyes is the Second or 'Architectural' Style which flourished in the 1st century. This style used images of colonnades and other architectural features to give an illusion of depth, with the view extending into the distance, and also featured figural characters and mythological scenes. The beautifully preserved villa at Boscoreale near Pompeii, from the very end of the Republican period, provides a number of magnificent architectural depictions from the bedroom of the owner, the little-known Publius Fannius Synistor (Figure 10). Perhaps the most famous set of images are those that gave their name to Pompeii's Villa of the Mysteries. Against a deep red background we see depicted rituals of the cult of Dionysus, as one woman is whipped and another dances naked clashing her cymbals (Figure 5). Such images offer a vision of Roman life far removed from the political and military narratives of our literary sources.

Sculpture in Rome had a long history, but as with painting the bulk of our evidence derives from the 2nd and 1st centuries. A few earlier terracotta statues survive, drawing on Etruscan models, but bronze and marble statues first came to Rome in any quantity after the sack of Syracuse in 211 and then Corinth in 146. Possession of such works became a mark of status and those who could not possess originals commissioned copies, creating a new

10. Second Style painting, from the bedroom of a villa at Boscoreale

industry that furnished the luxury villas. These Roman copies have proved highly valuable to scholars seeking to reconstruct lost Greek masterpieces such as the Diskobolos ('Discus-Thrower') of Myron and Polykleitos' Doryphoros ('Spear-Bearer'). They also attest again to Rome's deep-rooted admiration for Greek culture.

Even in the field of sculpture, however, the Romans were far more than passive emulators of the Greeks. Sculpture, and particularly the portraits of living individuals, had a special significance in Roman life. The wax images of a noble man's ancestors were held in the *atrium* of his house and carried during funeral processions, a further inspiration to emulate the achievements of the past. Roman marble portraits reflect the importance placed on such images as representative of traditional Roman virtues. In contrast to the classical Greek ideals of symmetry and youthful beauty, Roman portraits depict older mature men with lined battle-hardened faces, symbolizing Roman *virtus* and *auctoritas*. This characteristically Roman style of portraiture is often described as 'veristic', although the features shown still reflect an ideal as much as a specific individual's true likeness. Two of the earliest Republican portraits that can be identified with certainty are the busts of Pompeius and Caesar (Figure 11). The broad face of Pompeius Magnus, his frontal hairstyle recalling that of Alexander the Great, contrasts to the angular, aristocratic Julius Caesar.

In a much-quoted passage from Virgil's *Aeneid*, Aeneas' father Anchises prophesied Rome's destiny:

> Others shall hammer forth more delicately a breathing likeness out of bronze, coax living faces from the marble, plead causes with more skill, plot with their gauge the movements in the sky, and tell the rising of the constellations. But you, Roman, must remember that you have to guide the nations by your authority, for this is to be your skill, to graft tradition onto peace, to show mercy to the conquered, and to wage war until the haughty are brought low.

Anchises does not do justice to the Roman cultural achievement. Republican Rome would never rival the sheer breadth of the Greek genius, which the Romans themselves recognized and admired. Nevertheless, the Republic possessed its own genius, not only for conquest and government but for literature and art. Drawing on influences from many directions, the writings of Plautus and Cicero and the paintings of Pompeii reflect Roman values and reveal the living Roman world. Without that Republican legacy there would have been no golden age of Augustan culture, which in turn paved the way for the monumental splendour of the Roman Empire.

Chapter 8
The last years

Few periods of history have proved more compelling for later generations than the last traumatic years of the Roman Republic. The greatest power that the ancient world had yet known collapsed upon itself in an orgy of bloodshed. The crises of the 2nd century undermined the Senate's collective authority and witnessed the first of the line of warlords who dominated the late Republic. Gaius Marius and Lucius Cornelius Sulla were succeeded by Marcus Licinius Crassus, Gnaeus Pompeius Magnus, and Gaius Julius Caesar, who together formed the First Triumvirate. After Crassus' death, the alliance of Pompeius and Caesar dissolved into civil war, from which Caesar emerged triumphant. His murder on the Ides of March 44 BC could not save the failing Republic. The desperate act of Marcus Junius Brutus and his fellow 'Liberators' only served to plunge Rome into another decade of civil strife. Finally, Caesar's adopted son Gaius Julius Caesar Octavianus defeated Marcus Antonius and Cleopatra at Actium in 31 BC, and four years later took the name Augustus as the Roman Republic gave way to the Roman Empire.

With hindsight, it is tempting to view the Republic's decline as almost predestined, an inexorable fall from a height that could not be sustained. No external danger played a decisive part in the events that unfolded. The conflicts sprang from within, from the struggles of Republican society and government to adjust to the demands of controlling an empire and from the very pressures of noble competition, *gloria*, and *dignitas* that had driven Rome's expansion. Private armies and ever-increasing riches raised the stakes, until one man possessed the *dignitas*, wealth, and military might to rule alone. Yet few historical narratives are truly inevitable, and even at the end men were prepared to die for the Republic and its ideals. The fall of the Republic is not a tale of fate but a very human story of ambition and self-sacrifice, genius and folly. It is this universal human quality that underlies the enduring appeal of the Republic's last years.

The setting and the rising sun

The first critical blow was struck by Sulla. When he marched on Rome in 88 BC to prevent the transfer of his command to his rival Gaius Marius, Sulla threatened the very nature of the Republic. Through his private army, the warlord possessed power that neither the Senate's collective authority nor the popular assemblies could resist. But after seizing Rome, Sulla did not set himself up as an autocrat. His immediate concern was to defeat Mithridates of Pontus, whose invasion of Roman Asia had triggered the crisis, and for five years Sulla turned his back on Roman politics to campaign in the east. In his absence, his opponents rallied. Although Marius died in 86 BC shortly after beginning his seventh consulship, Sulla returned to Italy in 83 BC to discover his enemies allied with the Samnites, old Roman foes who were the only Italians still fighting after the Social War. Sulla's response was to march on Rome once more. He was joined by Crassus and Pompeius, who had raised their own private armies, and with their aid Sulla crushed his foes in a bloody battle at the Colline Gate of Rome.

Sulla now ruled the Republic. In order to formalize his position he revived the old office of dictator, which had not been held since the Second Punic War. Unlike a traditional Roman dictator he took the office indefinitely, not for a maximum of six months, and

Map 7. The last century of the Republic

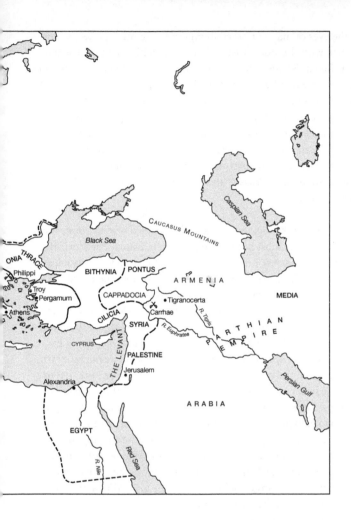

Black Sea

CAUCASUS MOUNTAINS

Caspian Sea

ONIA

THRACE

Philippi

BITHYNIA   PONTUS

ARMENIA

MEDIA

Troy

CAPPADOCIA

Pergamum

Tigranocerta

Carrhae

CILICIA

SYRIA

R. Tigris

Athens

R. Euphrates

PARTHIAN EMPIRE

CYPRUS

THE LEVANT

PALESTINE

Jerusalem

Persian Gulf

Alexandria

ARABIA

EGYPT

R. Nile

Red Sea

in the eyes of many of his contemporaries he was in effect a king. Armed with this authority, Sulla turned on his enemies. For the first time in Rome, proscriptions appeared – long lists of names of those who could be eliminated without appeal to justice. At least 80 senators and 2,600 *equites* were killed or exiled, and the true figures were probably higher. Sulla used the property confiscated from the dead to acquire the land that he had promised to his loyal soldiers (the town of Pompeii was a Sullan military colony). His supporters likewise exploited the proscriptions to buy up cheap estates, and Crassus and Pompeius became two of Rome's richest men.

The revival of the dictatorship and the dreaded proscriptions made Sulla one of the most hated men in Roman history. Paradoxical though it may seem, however, Sulla was at heart a true republican. Once his position was secure, he set out to restore the Senate to its pre-Gracchan authority. In order to do so, it was essential to prevent the exceptional careers of warlords like Marius and himself which challenged the Senate's collective harmony. Sulla therefore enforced the minimum ages at which each magistracy could be held and the proper stages of progression from quaestor to consul. He increased the number of quaestors to 20 and praetors to 8 to ease the burden of government, and reorganized the law courts under senatorial control. He also crippled the tribunes of the plebs who had caused the loss of his command in 88 BC. The tribunes' veto was limited to protecting individuals not interfering in matters of state, and any law proposed by a tribune had to have senatorial approval. What is more, no man who became a tribune could ever hold another political office, ensuring that ambitious men would avoid the position. In theory at least, there would never be another Tiberius or Gaius Gracchus.

His reforms complete, Sulla then stunned the Roman world in 79 BC by voluntarily resigning all offices and retiring into private life. For modern scholars, as for his contemporaries, Sulla remains an enigma. Ambitious and ruthless, he drove noble competition for *gloria* to new heights, yet dedicated his final years to the restoration of Republican values. He died in 78 BC, leaving his own epitaph: 'no better friend, no worse enemy'. But his efforts to strengthen the Republic would be in vain. The man who would destroy Sulla's reforms had already emerged before the former dictator's death: Gnaeus Pompeius 'Magnus'.

When Pompeius marched his three legions into Sulla's camp in 83 BC, he was just 23 years old and had never held public office. What he did have was wealth, ability, and charisma in abundance, with the confidence to match. During his early campaigns Pompeius won the nickname *adulescentulus carnifex* (the teenage butcher), but his preferred title was *Magnus*, an honorific that he awarded to himself in deliberate imitation of Alexander the Great. Pompeius Magnus was the very personification of what Sulla had sought to prevent, a man who challenged the established order and ignored the traditional path of Republican politics. Yet the Senate seemed helpless to check Pompeius' growing popularity and prestige. As he is said to have told Sulla, 'more men worship the rising than the setting sun'.

The 20 years that separated Sulla's death from the First Triumvirate marked a crucial phase in the decline and fall of the Republic. Sulla's reforms had in fact strengthened the Senate's hand. The structures of government and justice had been improved, and a foundation had been laid that might have led to the restoration of senatorial rule. What was required was a period of peace and stability to allow the reformed Republican system to become firmly established. Between the demands of noble competition and the sheer scale of Rome's empire, that period would never arrive. The course of Republican history in the 70s and 60s has to be traced through an unfolding sequence of crises that played directly into the hands of the warlords who controlled Rome's military machine.

Immediately upon Sulla's death, the consul Marcus Aemilius Lepidus attempted to seize sole power. It was only a minor disturbance, but it exposed the Senate's weakness, for there was no army which the existing magistrates could rally against the rebels. Pompeius, who just happened to be nearby, employed his own soldiers to crush Lepidus. He then won senatorial approval to go to Spain, where an old follower of Marius, the one-eyed Quintus Sertorius, was causing trouble. The struggle was fierce, for Sertorius proved a master of guerrilla warfare, but gradually Pompeius gained the upper hand and Sertorius was murdered by a traitor within his ranks. Victory gave Pompeius *gloria*, and his reorganization of Roman Spain brought him wealth and clients, before he returned to Rome in 71 BC.

During Pompeius' absence Italy had been wracked by a new crisis, the most famous slave revolt of ancient times. In 73 BC a Thracian gladiator escaped from the gladiatorial school of Capua with perhaps 70 men. His name was Spartacus. Gathering displaced farmers and slaves, he trained a force that defeated the consuls of 72 BC and ravaged much of central Italy from bases on and around Mount Vesuvius. The man chosen to hunt Spartacus down in 71 BC was Crassus. Systematic and ruthless, Crassus ground the revolt into the dust. Spartacus was killed in battle, and 6,000 of his followers were crucified along the length of the Appian Way from Capua to Rome. One small group did escape, only to be destroyed by the returning Pompeius. Spartacus' revolt would be immortalized in legend, but the humiliation of senatorial armies by renegade slaves further weakened a Senate now confronted with two rival warlords.

After the defeat of Spartacus, neither Pompeius nor Crassus disbanded their armies. With their soldiers camped outside Rome, the two men came to an agreement and stood together for election to the consulship. Crassus was a legal candidate of sufficient age and prior experience as a magistrate. Pompeius was still barely 36 and had not held any official positions at all. Nevertheless, their joint election in 70 BC was a foregone conclusion, and so Pompeius entered the Senate as consul in open contempt of Republican tradition. In their term of office the full powers of the tribunes of the plebs were restored, another blow to Sulla's efforts to focus authority upon the Senate. And a new crisis had emerged from a long-neglected quarter to disturb the fragile balance of power.

Piracy had been a danger in the Mediterranean since the earliest Roman times. In the 1st century that danger neared epidemic proportions, not least because Rome had crippled the old naval states of Carthage and Rhodes that had previously kept the pirates in check. By the early 60s Italian coastal towns were under attack, and the food supply on which Rome's growing population depended was threatened. The young Julius Caesar was captured by one pirate band while travelling in the east, paid an inflated ransom, and then returned to crucify his captors. Other Romans were less fortunate, and in 67 BC a law was passed offering Pompeius the command to end the pirate menace. The powers Pompeius was given were extraordinary: 124,000 men and 270 ships was the largest Republican force ever allocated to one man, and he held complete *imperium* at sea which extended up to 80 kilometres inland. Armed with such powers, Pompeius took less than five months to sweep the Mediterranean clear and capture the pirate strongholds of Cilicia in southern Asia Minor. He commemorated the feat in typical fashion by renaming the main city of Cilicia as Pompeiopolis, on the model of his hero Alexander.

Fresh from his phenomenal success, Pompeius then proceeded to take control of the ongoing war with Rome's most obdurate foe, Mithridates of Pontus. This struggle had been waged off and on for more than 20 years, and when Pompeius seized command Mithridates was already a beaten man. The king was finally killed in 63 BC, following which Pompeius took upon himself the reorganization of Rome's eastern territories. The coastal regions of Pontus, Bithynia, Cilicia, and Syria were at last declared Roman provinces, over a century after Rome had first extended its dominion east of Greece. Beyond those provinces were client kingdoms whose rulers acknowledged Roman superiority, including Judaea and Armenia. The latter in particular provided an important buffer between Rome and the Parthian Empire of Iran which emerged in the 1st century BC as Rome's chief rival. Taxation from the newly created provinces more than doubled Roman state revenues, but Pompeius too received huge sums from the kings who had paid to retain their thrones, as well as an enormous body of clients across the eastern Mediterranean. He returned to Rome the richest man in Roman history, and in 62 BC celebrated the most stunning triumph ever seen.

> In front of the procession were carried placards with the names of the countries over which he was triumphing. These were: Pontus, Armenia, Cappadocia, Paphlagonia, Media, Colchis, Iberia, Albania, Syria, Cilicia, Mesopotamia, Phoenicia, Palestine, Judaea, and Arabia. There was also the power of the pirates, overthrown both at sea and on land. In the course of these campaigns it was shown that he had captured no less than 1000 fortified places, nearly 900 cities, and 800 pirate ships; he had founded 39 cities.

How could anyone compete with such a triumph? The bar for Roman noble competition had been raised almost out of sight, and many in the Senate feared Pompeius' pre-eminence. The result was a stand-off. Upon his return, Pompeius requested senatorial ratification of his eastern reorganization and that land should be granted as promised to his veteran soldiers. He was supported by his old rival Crassus, who wished to exploit the taxes collected in those eastern regions. But Pompeius was opposed by a bloc of conservative senators led by the formidable Marcus Porcius Cato the Younger, who modelled himself on his great-grandfather Cato the Elder both in his moral integrity and in his rigid refusal to compromise. Pompeius was not prepared to resort to violence, fearing that he would earn the hatred bestowed on Sulla, and he lacked the political skill to achieve his ends. It was this impasse that opened the way for a hitherto relatively minor figure to enter centre stage: Gaius Julius Caesar.

Caesar and Pompeius

Born in 100 BC, Caesar was a scion of the famous Julian clan that traced its descent back through Romulus to Aeneas and the goddess Venus. This was an enormous source of *dignitas*, but the family was not politically prominent, and Caesar's early career was far more conventional than that of Pompeius. He held the usual junior offices at the usual ages, and his most striking achievement was to gain election in 63 BC as *pontifex maximus*, the head of the Roman state religion. After winning several minor campaigns in Spain, Caesar came to Rome in 60 BC to celebrate a triumph and seek election to the consulship. Forced by Cato and the conservatives to choose between his triumph and standing for election, Caesar preferred the latter and through a potent blend of political talent and personal charisma united the rivals Pompeius and Crassus behind him. In return for Caesar's promise to secure their desires, they provided the money and influence required to elect Caesar as consul for 59 BC.

Thus was created the First Triumvirate, an informal alliance between the three men sealed by the marriage of Pompeius to Caesar's daughter Julia. Caesar was duly elected consul, although his colleague was Marcus Calpurnius Bibulus, a friend of Cato and resolutely hostile. Unable to secure senatorial approval, Caesar took his laws to the popular assembly where, with the support of Pompeius and Crassus, they were passed. Bibulus retired from public life after what may politely be described as 'filth' was dumped on him in the Forum, and he remained at home where he declared that he was watching for evil omens. This religious intervention technically rendered Caesar's laws illegal as they were passed without divine approval, a charge that would return to haunt Caesar in later years. For the moment, the First Triumvirate ruled supreme. Caesar's laws gave the required land to Pompeius' veterans and ratified the eastern settlement and tax contracts. His term in office complete, Caesar then set out for Gaul in search of wealth and *gloria* of his own.

> All Gaul is divided into three parts, inhabited respectively by the
> Belgae, the Aquitani, and a people who call themselves Celts,
> though we call them Gauls.

So Caesar began his *Commentaries on the Gallic War*, the
narrative (written in third person) that he composed to justify and
celebrate his conquest of Gaul. The popularity of the
Commentaries has contributed to a romantic image of Caesar's
conquests, notably his struggles with the Gallic chieftain
Vercingetorix who defeated Caesar at Gergovia before succumbing
at Alesia. Seen in a harsher light the Gallic War might accurately
be described as genocide, for in the course of a decade Caesar
killed and enslaved approximately one million people. His actions
were also significant for marking the first penetration of Roman
power across the Rhine into Germany and over the Channel into
Britain, though with little practical effect. What the conquests did
unquestionably confirm was Caesar's ambition and military
prowess. He now had the *gloria*, the wealth, and the veteran army
needed to challenge Pompeius' supremacy.

Back in Rome, trouble was brewing. Cicero, who had been driven
into temporary exile due to his opposition to the triumvirs,
worked together with the senatorial conservatives to split
Pompeius from Caesar. As the First Triumvirate began to weaken,
Caesar interrupted his Gallic campaigns to attend a meeting of the
triumvirs at the Conference of Lucca in 56 BC. There they renewed
their alliance. Caesar's command in Gaul was extended, while
Pompeius and Crassus shared the consulship again before Crassus
in his turn set out to win *gloria* in the east. But the cracks were
beginning to show. The successful marriage of Pompeius and Julia
was ended by Julia's tragic death in childbirth in 54 BC, breaking a
vital bond between Caesar and Pompeius. Crassus, who provided
the balance between his more ambitious colleagues, launched an
assault upon the Parthian Empire, an enemy whose true strength
the Romans were yet to comprehend. He and his army were
massacred at Carrhae in 53 BC by the Parthian combination of

11. Portrait busts of (a) Pompeius and (b) Caesar

heavy cavalry and horse-archers. The Roman world began to divide into two camps, for even Rome's empire was not large enough to contain both Pompeius and Caesar.

The clash of the two warlords, which marked the beginning of the end for the Republic, was a very Roman civil war. It was not a war fought over patriotism or rival visions for Rome's future. It was a struggle for power, *gloria*, and *dignitas*, the selfish principles of the Roman elite, and marked the culmination of the self-destructive Roman competitive ethos. As Caesar's ten-year campaign in Gaul drew to a close, his enemies gathered to condemn him. Pompeius, fully aware of the threat that Caesar posed to his pre-eminence, allied with Cato and the conservatives to champion the 'Republican' cause. Like Sulla a generation before, when faced with the choice between war and political oblivion, Caesar chose war. Appealing to his soldiers to defend his *dignitas*, on 11 January 49 BC Caesar crossed the Rubicon River into Roman Italy with the immortal words *alea iacta est* ('the die is cast'). Looking back a century later under the emperor Nero, the Roman poet Lucan simply declared 'Caesar would accept no superior, Pompeius would accept no equal'.

Over the five years that followed, violence spread to all corners of the Mediterranean. Pompeius withdrew eastward to rally his supporters, and when Caesar came in pursuit the two men at last met in battle in 48 BC at Pharsalus in central Greece. Caesar was outnumbered two to one, but his troops were veterans and he personally led the flank attack that routed Pompeius' army. Among the prisoners who received Caesar's pardon were Cicero and Brutus. Pompeius fled to Egypt, where he was murdered on the beach at the orders of the king, the 13-year-old Ptolemy XIII. Caesar had the murderers executed and formed an alliance with Ptolemy's 17-year-old sister Cleopatra VII (who, according to legend, was smuggled into Caesar's tent inside a rolled carpet). Ptolemy XIII was killed, and Caesar left Cleopatra to rule Egypt with her younger brother Ptolemy XIV, who quickly died, and a newborn son whom she named Caesarion.

Although Pompeius was dead, Caesar still faced many enemies. Some posed little danger, such as Mithridates' son Pharnaces of Pontus who in 47 BC was crushed in less than a week, a feat Caesar commemorated with the laconic words *veni, vidi, vici* ('I came, I saw, I conquered'). Far more threatening were the surviving defenders of the Republican cause, now led by Cato the Younger. Caesar defeated one army at Thapsus in North Africa in 46 BC and Cato chose suicide rather than face Caesar's clemency, a martyr to the Republic which many Romans would later believe died with him. Even then Pompeius' former supporters rallied again in Spain, and the Battle of Munda in 45 BC was the hardest and bloodiest battle of the war. Caesar's victory finally confirmed his status as the sole ruler of the Roman world.

The Ides of March

The destruction of the civil war wreaked havoc on the Republic. The provinces were in disarray and the Senate had lost any authority as the governing body of Rome. It fell upon Caesar to rebuild what he had helped to destroy. During his surprisingly brief period of sole rule, he laid the foundations for a number of key developments in the subsequent history of the Roman Empire. Provincial administration and taxation were reorganized, and Roman citizenship was extended outside Italy to areas of Gaul, Spain, and beyond. Colonies were founded to revive derelict cities like Carthage and Corinth, and to settle Caesar's disbanded veterans. Within Rome, Caesar created a solar calendar of 365.25 days to replace Rome's inaccurate lunar calendar, and began a programme of public works to provide employment and glorify the city and himself.

Few of Caesar's reforms provoked direct opposition. It was the means by which he expressed his power that inspired hatred. In order to maintain control, Caesar insisted upon retaining the dictatorship even longer than had the despised Sulla. A decree that Caesar would hold the office for ten years in 45 was superseded in early 44 by the announcement that he would be dictator perpetual, an utterly un-Roman concept that suggests Caesar had lost touch with Republican feeling. Magistrates were no longer selected through election, but were nominated by Caesar up to five years in advance of their term in office. The Senate still voted on decisions, but Caesar had already made them, and Cicero complained that his name was added to decrees that he had never seen. The month Quinctilus became Julius (July), and the rumours that Caesar wished to become *rex* (king) could not be dispelled, even when Caesar publicly refused the crown offered to him by Marcus Antonius at the Lupercalia festival in February 44 BC. In a culture in which the title *rex* had been hated for centuries, Caesar was all too blatantly an autocrat.

In the opening months of 44 BC Caesar was preparing a great campaign against the Parthians to avenge Crassus and escape the tense atmosphere of Rome. His planned departure gave his enemies a date by which they had to strike. Caesar knew well that he was hated. His wife Calpurnia dreamed of his murder, and the soothsayer Spurinna told him to beware the Ides of March. On his journey to a Senate meeting on that fateful day (15 March), 'Caesar met the soothsayer and greeted him jestingly with the words: "the Ides of March have come". To which the soothsayer replied in a soft voice: "yes, but they have not yet gone"' (Plutarch). Caesar was surrounded in the Senate house and hacked to death, falling under a statue of Pompeius that he had restored.

Some 60 men or more knew of the conspiracy against Caesar, eloquent testimony to the depth of hostility he had aroused. Cicero, who feared Caesar as much as he admired him, hailed his death in a chilling letter as 'the most gorgeous banquet'. The figurehead of the 'Liberators', as they called themselves, was Marcus Junius Brutus, the son-in-law of Cato the Younger and a descendant of the Brutus who had expelled the kings in 510 BC. It was to him that Caesar addressed his last words, *kai su teknon* ('and you, my child'), replaced in Shakespeare's play by *et tu Brute*. Brutus had received Caesar's clemency after Pharsalus and was earmarked for future office, suggesting that he was not driven purely by ambition. This cannot be said of all his comrades, whose motives varied widely from personal hatred to a desire to compete for the offices and honours that Caesar now controlled. What none of the Liberators possessed, however, was any vision of what the future would hold once Caesar was killed. Possibly they simply hoped that the old Republic would return. But that Republic was already dead, and Caesar's murder merely left a vacuum of power for others to fill.

Caesar had accurately predicted that his death would begin another civil war. Brutus and the Liberators were driven from Rome by Marcus Antonius, Caesar's second in command. But

Antonius in turn was challenged by the appearance of Gaius Octavius, Caesar's 18-year-old grand-nephew, who by the terms of Caesar's will was adopted as Caesar's son and heir, Gaius Julius Caesar Octavianus. Together with Marcus Aemilius Lepidus, Antonius and Octavianus formed the Second Triumvirate. Cicero was one of the victims of their rise to power in 43 BC, and in 42 the Liberators were defeated in two battles at Philippi in Greece and Brutus killed himself. Yet the Second Triumvirate was no more stable than its predecessor had been. The ineffectual Lepidus was pushed aside, and once again the Roman world became polarized, between Octavianus in Italy and Antonius with his new ally Cleopatra of Egypt. Defeated at the naval battle of Actium in 31 BC, Antonius and Cleopatra fled to Egypt where they too committed suicide. The ruler of the Roman world was Octavianus, who four years later took the title Augustus.

The Roman Republic spanned almost 500 years. A story that began with the expulsion of a king ended with the rise of an emperor. The city of Rome was transformed from a small town fighting for survival in Italy to the mistress of a vast Mediterranean empire whose dominion was only threatened by conflict from within. Yet the triumph and tragedy of the Republic are inseparably intertwined. The Republic's unique constitution gave Rome stability and direction under the collective authority of the Senate, while the social pressures of noble competition and desire for *gloria* drove Rome towards expansion. But expansion unleashed social, political, and economic forces that the Republic could not contain, and as the stakes of competition rose, power passed into the hands of warlords whose rivalry descended into civil war. Nevertheless, the Republic's story does not end with the futility and bloodshed of Pompeius and Caesar, Antonius and Octavianus. Rome's dominion over the Mediterranean would endure for centuries to come, an empire rooted in the achievements of the Republic. And even beyond Rome, the Republic's legacy has remained an ideal and a warning for later generations down to the present day.

Chapter 9
The afterlife of the Republic

Two millennia have passed since the Roman Republic fell, yet its legacy has endured. The Roman Empire which emerged from the ruins continued to draw upon Republican traditions, even as imperial autocracy replaced collective senatorial rule. The gradual conversion of the Empire to Christianity added a further element, with respect for Rome's antiquity balanced by condemnation of its pagan origins, a tension clearly visible in Augustine of Hippo's masterwork the *City of God*. Over the centuries that followed the Republic's influence faded, until the great revival of classical literature and art now known as the Renaissance. From the political philosophy of Machiavelli to Shakespeare's plays, the ideals and lessons, heroes and villains of Republican history were reborn for a new world. This new appreciation of the Roman past acquired greater significance in the turbulent 18th century as the great revolutions in America and France drew inspiration from visions of a Republican utopia. And still today the Roman Republic pervades modern Western culture from intellectual discourse to film and television, impacting on our lives in ways that many are not even aware.

From Republic to Empire

At the age of nineteen on my own responsibility and at my own expense I raised an army, with which I successfully championed the liberty of the republic when it was oppressed by the tyranny of a faction.

The opening words of the *Res Gestae*, the memorial inscription carved on Augustus' mausoleum, immortalized his self-image as the defender of the Republic. Augustus rejected any title that might suggest autocratic rule, and preferred the more traditional designation *princeps*, first citizen. In reality, Augustus was an emperor and the structures that had governed the Republic existed solely in name. The Senate no longer held authority but endorsed Augustus' requests, the annual magistrates were nominated by the *princeps* not elected by the assemblies, and the army answered to the emperor who represented the state. By Augustus' death in AD 14 imperial rule was firmly established and the Republic had given way to the Empire.

Yet Augustus' image, the so-called façade of the Principate, is itself confirmation of the ongoing hold the Republic retained on Rome. He had learned from the fate of Julius Caesar, whose openly autocratic leadership led directly to his assassination. Augustus treated the Senate with respect, defended Republican social values, and championed morality and religion. Thus he placated a people exhausted by a generation of civil war and prepared to accept power presented in traditional terms. Augustus' immediate successors were forced to make similar concessions. Every Roman emperor of the 1st century AD who aspired to naked autocracy was cut down, from Caligula and Nero to Domitian. A *princeps* could not rule without acknowledging Rome's Republican past.

In the patterns of everyday life, the transition from Republic to Empire wrought gradual but significant change. A time-traveller who passed from the early 1st century BC to the late 1st century AD might have been struck by the similarities as much as the differences. Styles of dress, housing design, and the distinctions of class and gender had altered little. Republican literature continued to be read, Republican art was adapted to imperial service. Yet there were also new elements, for what did change dramatically under the Empire was the definition of who was entitled to bear the name Roman. Under the Republic, Roman citizenship was granted to other Italians only after the Social War and to non-Italians only as a gesture of exceptional favour. Through the 1st and 2nd centuries AD Roman identity spread across the Mediterranean, until in the 3rd century citizenship was extended throughout the Empire. In this increasingly Romanized world, Republican traditions lacked relevance outside Rome itself. The newly Roman populations of Gaul and Spain or the Greek eastern provinces had no desire to celebrate their unsuccessful struggles with Republican armies. Knowledge of the Republic declined with the passing years, although important to members of noble families who as late as the 4th century took pride in claiming descent (however fictitious) from the great Republican heroes.

The City of God

By the 4th century, a new element had taken firm root within the Roman world. In the years following the conversion in AD 312 of Constantine, the first Christian emperor, Christianity expanded to become the dominant religion of the Empire. For the Christians, Rome's Republican history was both an attraction and a challenge. Many Christians took great pride in their Roman heritage, particularly those from the educated elite. But they had turned away from the ancient gods, who according to Roman tradition had given Rome dominion. The Gothic sack of Rome in AD 410, the first time that the city had suffered such a catastrophe in eight centuries, brought these tensions to a new height. Had Rome fallen to the wrath of the gods whom the Christians had abandoned? It was against this background that Augustine of Hippo (AD 354–430) composed what would become the most influential early Christian interpretation of the Roman Republic, which he incorporated within his *magnum opus*, the *City of God*.

Augustine's vision of Republican history was very different from that of Livy or Cicero. Against those who still attributed the rise and fall of the Republic to Roman morality and the ancient gods, Augustine condemned the early Romans and their gods alike. How could the demons whom those Romans worshipped reward their followers for virtue, when they themselves were renowned for vice? Jupiter was a serial adulterer, Venus abandoned her husband Vulcan to flirt with Mars. The myriad gods of Republican religion were no more than a laughing stock, and had failed to protect Rome from the disasters wrought by Pyrrhus and Hannibal. Nor did early Rome deserve its reputation as a golden age of virtue. Roman history began in blood, with Romulus' murder of Remus and the Rape of the Sabine Women. Lucretia killed herself out of pride not the humble modesty of a Christian woman. The Romans proclaimed their *fides* and yet brought destruction upon their allies, and obsession with *dignitas* and *gloria* drove the lust for power that plunged the later Republic into civil war. Augustine thus took the traditional values of the Republic and turned them back against the Romans, who only learned true virtue with the coming of Christ.

Nevertheless, Augustine did concede a certain pre-eminence to the Roman Republic. Like the Romans of earlier generations, he too attributed the conquest of Rome's empire to divine providence, that of the Christian God. Why had God allowed pagan Rome to hold authority over the ancient world? In Augustine's eyes, God entrusted dominion:

> To those men, in preference to all others, who served their country for the sake of honour, praise and glory, who looked to find that glory in their country's safety above their own and who suppressed greed for money and many other faults in favour of that one fault of theirs, the love of praise.

The Roman desire for *gloria*, if not in itself a virtue, kept more grievous vices in check and so earned God's favour. The Republic's heroes had qualities which Christians should learn from and excel. Cincinnatus came from his plough to take on the dictatorship and then returned to his poverty; Gaius Fabricius rejected the bribes of Pyrrhus.

> If we do not display in the service of the most glorious City of God the qualities of which the Romans, after their fashion, gave us something of a model in their pursuit of the glory of their earthly city, then we ought to feel the prick of shame. If we do display these virtues, we must not be infected with pride.

As just reward for their qualities, the Romans were exalted in the earthly realm. But they will not receive the highest reward that awaits Christians in heaven. The Roman Republic, like all worldly domains, was temporary, unlike the true and eternal kingdom of God.

Over the centuries that followed Augustine, knowledge of Republican history dwindled. In the east the Roman Empire survived as the Empire of Byzantium, and Byzantine writers continued to show interest in the Roman past whose traditions they claimed to preserve. But in the post-Roman west the heroes and stories of the Republic were superseded by those of the Old and New Testaments, just as the writings of Augustine and other Church fathers took the place of Plautus, Catullus, and Cicero. The Vatican Library in Rome preserves a manuscript originally held in the Bobbio monastery in northern Italy. There, probably in the late 7th century, an anonymous monk over-wrote what is now the only extant copy of Cicero's *De Re Publica* with one of countless versions of Augustine's *Commentary on the Psalms*. The fragmentary survival of Cicero's great political treatise, and the loss of so many Republican works beyond recall, is a sad testimony to the reduced state into which the Republic's memory fell in the medieval age.

Machiavelli and Shakespeare

Revival of Western interest in the Roman Republic and the world of the ancients came with the beginning of the Renaissance in the

14th century. For the Italian city-states like Florence in which admiration for classical art and literature first took hold, the rise of Rome had a special resonance. Italian scholars like Petrarch (1304–74) set out to collect the scattered remnants of Republican culture, and Republican ideals were adapted to serve new social and political models. As the Renaissance spread throughout Europe, ancient Rome was reinterpreted in many different forms to fill widely varying needs. The sheer diversity of that process of adaptation is embodied in the writings of two men from contrasting extremes of the Renaissance: the political philosophy of the Florentine Niccolò Machiavelli and the plays of the Englishman William Shakespeare.

The name of Niccolò Machiavelli (1469–1527) is usually associated today with the cynical and devious exercise of authority encapsulated by the word 'machiavellian'. *The Prince*, his most famous work, advises a ruler on how to achieve and maintain power. Machiavelli was also a leading thinker on the nature of republican government, particularly in regard to his own city of Florence, and his search for a model republic inevitably drew him to ancient Rome. As he declared near the beginning of his *Discourses on the First Ten Books of Livy*:

> Those who read how the city of Rome had its beginning, who were its founders, and what its ordinances and laws, will not be astonished that so much excellence was maintained in it through many ages, or that it grew afterwards to be so great an Empire.

Despite its title, Machiavelli's work covers the whole span of the Republic, not merely Livy's early books, and through Republican examples offers practical guidance on how states and statesmen should act. Those examples range from the Conflict of the Orders and the tension between aristocratic and popular government to military advice drawn from the careers of Hannibal and Scipio Africanus. Seen through the pragmatic eyes of Machiavelli rather than the religious vision of Augustine, the Roman Republic acquired a new significance as a source of inspiration amidst the complex politics of Renaissance Italy.

Of course, Machiavelli was fully aware of the flaw in upholding Rome as a model Republic. Rome's success had brought its own downfall, its social and political structures unable to cope with the conquest of an empire. For Machiavelli, the explanation was straightforward.

> If we examine well the course of Roman history, we shall find two causes leading to the break-up of that republic: one, the dissensions which arose in connection with the agrarian laws; the other, the prolongation of military commands.

From these causes, the Republic faced conflict with the people and lost control over the nobles and their armies. Machiavelli mourned Rome's loss of freedom with the rise of the emperors but offered no cure, for such was the price Rome paid for its triumphs. A republic, he argued, had to choose whether like Rome its aim was expansion or whether it preferred self-preservation like ancient Sparta or contemporary Venice. Machiavelli's choice was clear. Perhaps those states that rejected expansion might last a little longer and avoid the conflicts that beset the Roman Republic. But this was not the path to glory. All states either rise or fall, and it is better to accept the challenge of dissension and ambition, 'looking on them as evils which cannot be escaped if we would arrive at the greatness of Rome'.

The theatres of Elizabethan England were a very different world from the political councils of Machiavelli's Florence. Yet the Roman Republic proved no less an attraction for William Shakespeare (1564–1616), whose plays have been as influential as any modern media in bringing ancient Rome to life. Shakespeare's Roman interests reflected the currents of his time (the earliest known play of his rival Christopher Marlowe was *Dido, Queen of Carthage*, a work inspired by Virgil's *Aeneid*). But it is Shakespeare's works that best preserve the Elizabethan vision of the Roman past. Three Shakespearean plays are based on events from Republican history: *Julius Caesar* (1599), *Antony and Cleopatra* (1606), and *Coriolanus* (1608). All three drew heavily on Plutarch's *Lives*, translated into English by Sir Thomas North in 1579, although Plutarch was not Shakespeare's only source. *Titus Andronicus* (1592) and *Cymbeline* (1610) likewise take place in Roman contexts but are set after the Republic's fall, while *The Comedy of Errors* (1594) unfolds in Greek Asia Minor but is based upon the Roman comedies of Plautus. In addition to his plays, Shakespeare also depicted the events that led to the creation of the Republic in a narrative poem: *The Rape of Lucrece* (1593–4).

Unlike Machiavelli, Shakespeare had little interest in the Republic as an ideal state. England was a monarchy and its kings lent their names to many of Shakespeare's finest historical plays. The social and political tensions of Republican Rome, however, struck a powerful chord in contemporary debates over popular representation, aristocratic privilege, and autocratic power. Shakespeare's choice of subject for his Republican plays reflected those debates as well as the poet's keen eye for character and dramatic potential. The centuries of Roman expansion and relative political stability were ignored. Instead, Shakespeare concentrated his efforts around the two poles of the Republic's birth and its decline and fall.

Shakespeare first explored the Republic's origins in poetic form in *The Rape of Lucrece* (Lucretia), concluding with Brutus' oath of vengeance and the revolt against Tarquin Superbus. Almost two decades later, Shakespeare returned to that theme by exploiting the probably legendary figure of Gaius Marcius Coriolanus. Exiled from Rome by his rivals, Coriolanus allied with Rome's enemies to exact revenge. His attack upon Rome was only averted by the appeals of his mother and wife, after which he was killed by his new allies as a traitor to all. Shakespeare set his *Coriolanus* amidst the opening stages of the Conflict of the Orders, and the contrast between the arrogant aristocracy and the fickle favour of the masses had an obvious resonance for his audience. Rather than the historical issue of debt enslavement, the poor in Shakespeare's version are angered by the nobility's hoarding of grain, a complaint that had provoked bloody riots in the so-called Midland Revolt shortly before *Coriolanus* was composed. The tragic hero himself is trapped between the different factions and his own pride, the tensions exposed by his actions left unresolved by his death.

To modern audiences *Coriolanus* is one of Shakespeare's less memorable plays. This can hardly be said of *Julius Caesar* and *Antony and Cleopatra*. Taken together, the two plays narrate the period from the dictatorship of Caesar to the triumph of Octavianus (the future Augustus). Shakespeare again had no abiding interest in the underlying causes that led to the Republic's fall. But the murder of Caesar raised the twin questions of political succession and the legitimacy of tyrannicide which were the focus of great controversy in Tudor and Stuart England. For Shakespeare those questions intertwined with the humanity of his characters, whose complex motives are not Roman or Elizabethan as much as they are universal. His achievement is encapsulated in the opening of Antony's famous speech at Caesar's funeral.

> Friends! Romans! Countrymen! Lend me your ears.
> I come to bury Caesar, not to praise him.
> The evil that men do lives after them;
> The good is oft interred with their bones:
> So let it be with Caesar. The noble Brutus
> Hath told you Caesar was ambitious.
> If it were so, it was a grievous fault,
> And grievously hath Caesar answered it.
> Here, under leave of Brutus and the rest –
> For Brutus is an honourable man,
> So are they all, all honourable men –
> Come I to speak in Caesar's funeral.
> He was my friend: faithful and just to me.

12. Marlon Brando as Mark Antony in the 1953 film adaptation of Shakespeare's *Julius Caesar*

> But Brutus says he was ambitious,
> And Brutus is an honourable man.
> (*Julius Caesar*, Act 3, Scene 2)

It is a tribute to Shakespeare's genius that audiences have never agreed on whether *Julius Caesar* is more favourable to the character of Caesar or Brutus. Caesar's ambition is a very Roman quality, as too is the obsession with Brutus' honour or *dignitas*. But these are also universal values, no less than Antony's loyalty to his friend and later the crowd's horror at the sight of Caesar's mutilated body. Brutus *is* an honourable man, praised on his death as 'the noblest Roman of them all'. Yet his honour drove him to the murder of a man who had treated him like a son. Shakespeare's Brutus is a far more ambiguous and human figure than that of Plutarch. The same can be said of the protagonists of *Antony and Cleopatra*, although neither the passionate luxury-loving couple nor the calculating Octavianus are as appealing or tragic as Brutus. Whatever complaints a purist lacking in romance might level against his historical accuracy, Shakespeare brought his ancient

Romans to life in a manner that few have ever rivalled and in this lies the secret to the enduring popularity of his Roman plays.

Republic and revolution

The Renaissance's impact upon the memory of the Roman Republic was profound. Nowhere was this more apparent than in the dramatic years of the Age of Revolutions in the 18th and 19th centuries. The revival in knowledge of the Roman past helped to fuel the rising tide of hostility to absolute monarchy that spread across Europe and the New World. The Roman Republic offered an ideal for government without kings, a state where (it was believed) freedom had been safeguarded by the rule of law under a sovereign people and their elected magistrates. Thomas Hobbes in his *Leviathan* (1651) already associated the English Civil War with the influence of Cicero and 'the opinions of the Romans, who were taught to hate monarchy'. In the 18th century republican ideas drawing upon Roman models gathered force in the United States and France, with vastly contrasting fortunes.

A 21st-century visitor to Washington, DC may still behold the influence of the Roman Republic on the Founding Fathers of the United States of America. When the new federal capital was founded in 1791, the very landmarks of the city were renamed in honour of Rome. Goose Creek became Tiber Creek, Jenkins Hill became Capitol Hill, and the meeting place of the United States Congress was the Capitol itself, recalling Rome's Temple of Jupiter Optimus Maximus. Such references were familiar to all those who had taken part in the debates that accompanied the framing of the United States Constitution. Many had published their arguments under Republican pseudonyms like Brutus, Cato, and Cincinnatus. The *Federalist Papers* (1787–8) of James Madison and Alexander Hamilton, the two men chiefly responsible for drafting the Constitution, were written under the name Publius in invocation of Publius Valerius Publicola, who had stood alongside the original Brutus when the Republic was founded.

These allusions were more than mere rhetorical flourishes. For the men who first shaped the United States, the Roman Republic offered a practical model to which they could turn for guidance. One such man was John Adams, who in 1787 published his great treatise, the *Defence of the Constitutions of Government of the United States of America*. Adams, who succeeded George Washington as the second president of the United States (1797–1801), believed strongly in a balanced constitution for which Rome provided the historical archetype. His favoured spokesman was Cicero, whose vision of republican government Adams hailed in his preface:

> As all the ages of the world have not produced a greater statesman and philosopher united in the same character, his authority should have great weight. His decided opinion in favour of three branches is founded on a reason that is unchangeable; the laws, which are the only possible rule, measure, and security of justice, can be sure of protection, for any course of time, in no other form of government: and the very name of a republic implies, that the property of the people should be represented in the legislature, and decide the rule of justice.

The three branches of government in Cicero's Republic were the magistrates, the Senate, and the popular assemblies. In Adams's constitution, those branches became the president (who held the executive power of the consuls), the Senate (which ratified treaties and acted as a check on the other branches), and the House of Representatives (which approved laws and declarations of war). Like Machiavelli, Adams and his contemporaries knew that the Roman Republic had ultimately failed. Their solution was twofold. For reasons of practicality and to avoid what many regarded as the tyranny of simple majority democracy, the elected House of Representatives replaced the assemblies. The general populace were thus excluded from any collective role in government, a measure that the senatorial elitist Cicero would have heartily approved. Secondly, and again in accordance with Cicero's ideals, the checks and balances of the system were strengthened. If any one branch or person gained excessive power, as had occurred in the fall of Republican Rome, the other branches could combine to contain them. The new United States thus learned the lessons of the past, and achieved the stability that Rome itself had won and then lost.

Republicanism in France never acquired the same coherence or stability as in the United States, but nevertheless drew on many of the same classical models. In the years before the Revolution broke out in 1789, there was strong French interest in the Roman Republic. The Baron de Montesquieu's *De l'esprit des lois* (*The Spirit of the Laws*) was published in 1748 and exerted considerable influence on the American Founding Fathers, particularly for his insistence on the separation of the executive, legislative, and judicial functions of government. The lessons that he drew from Roman history, however, were very different. According to Montesquieu, 'the government of Rome, after the expulsion of the kings, should naturally have been a democracy'. Yet this did not occur. The senatorial nobility continued to hold authority and, as Rome's empire expanded, individual wealth and ambition led to tyranny. 'It is natural', Montesquieu concluded, 'for a republic to have only a small territory; otherwise it cannot long subsist'. A large republic such as Rome must inevitably become corrupt and fall into despotism, abandoning the love of virtue that Montesquieu defined as the principle upon which all republican government must rest.

Montesquieu's vision of Republican Rome was adopted and refined in the work that more than any other inspired the ideals of the French Revolution: *Du contrat social* (*The Social Contract*) of Jean-Jacques Rousseau (1762). In his search for the ideal state, Rousseau looked to Rome to understand 'how the freest and most powerful people on earth exercised their supreme power'. His emphasis upon liberty secured through the rule of law closely paralleled the arguments of his American contemporaries. But Rousseau placed a far higher value on popular sovereignty and on the need to maintain public morality to avoid the decline into despotism prophesied by Montesquieu. Rousseau's chief aim in *Du contrat social* was therefore to encourage citizens to live the lives of virtue that his vision of republican government required. It was on these terms that Rousseau held up the Roman Republic as a symbol that his own times might aspire to emulate. Under the Republic, Rousseau believed:

> The people were then not only Sovereign, but also magistrate and judge. The Senate was only a subordinate tribunal, to temper and concentrate the government, and the consuls themselves, though they were patricians, first magistrates, and absolute generals in war, were in Rome itself no more than presidents of the people.

This popular sovereignty was in turn preserved by Roman morality. The primary characteristic that Rousseau ascribed to the Romans was virtue, just as the ancient Jews were characterized by religion and the Carthaginians by commerce. Even the Republic's decline into anarchy and tyranny failed to compromise Rousseau's exaltation of the Roman people, who 'never ceased to elect magistrates, to pass laws, to judge cases, and to carry through business both public and private'. Blame for the Republic's fall Rousseau placed squarely on 'the abuse of aristocracy' which led to civil war.

Neither Rousseau's interpretation of Roman politics nor his admiration for Roman virtue can stand up to serious historical criticism. But his influence was profound, his vision of ancient Rome no less compelling for French audiences than that of John Adams for the Founding Fathers. Indeed, Rousseau and Adams reveal through their contrasting interpretations of Rome the diverging paths of American and French republicanism that would play out in the French Revolution. Rather than Adams's Ciceronian pattern of checks and balances, the French revolutionaries followed Rousseau in championing popular sovereignty and public morality. The attempt to create the 'republic of virtue' culminated in the Terror of Robespierre, and in barely ten years France re-enacted five

13. Jacques-Louis David, *The Intervention of the Sabine Women* (1799)

centuries of Roman history. The overthrow of the monarchy was succeeded by a Republic that disintegrated into anarchy and eventually autocracy. Nevertheless, Rome's appeal still endured, immortalized in Jacques-Louis David's *The Intervention of the Sabine Women* (1799), unveiled in the year that Napoleon Bonaparte seized power as the First Consul of France.

From Roman emperors and Church fathers to the Renaissance and the Age of Revolutions, different generations reinterpreted the memory of the Republic to serve the needs of a changing world. It was an ongoing process that has continued without interruption down to the present day. In the 19th century, the prevailing interpretation of Republican expansion focused around the idea of 'defensive imperialism'. Rome's recurring wars were not attributed to aggression or greed, but were fought to protect Rome and its allies. Such an interpretation found support in Livy and other Roman sources. But 'defensive imperialism' also justified the imperial powers of contemporary Europe, who represented the conquest of their overseas empires in similar terms. The collapse of those empires was followed in the second half of the 20th century by an increasing emphasis upon Roman militancy and the pressures that drove Rome to expand. More recent commentators have likewise shown a greater interest in Republican life outside the traditional spheres of politics and war. Roman family ties, gender roles, and social and religious values all hold new relevance to observers from the early 21st century.

The Roman Republic continues to pervade Western culture. Some of the influences are so deeply rooted that they can easily be ignored. The networks of Roman roads and cities that spread across much of Europe during the imperial centuries first took shape under the Republic, as too did the spread of Latin as the foundation for the later Romance languages. Republican terms and concepts feature prominently in our political debates, Republican words and images inspire modern authors and artists. And the drama of Republican history has never ceased to strike a chord in our imagination, be it the Gallic Sack of Rome and Hannibal crossing the Alps or Julius Caesar on the banks of the Rubicon and the Ides of March.

14. Ciarán Hinds as Julius Caesar in the HBO/BBC series, *Rome*

Every subsequent generation that has turned to the Roman Republic for inspiration has revealed something of their own character in the lessons they have sought to learn. Today, looking back across over two millennia, it is the fall of the Republic that once again captures the public eye. The triumphant years of Roman expansion feature only rarely in film and television, producers and audiences alike favouring the Republic's violent and tragic end. From the classic Kirk Douglas film *Spartacus* (1960) to the BBC series *Rome* (2005), the attraction of the final years of the Republic to those who aspire to bring the Roman past to life is obvious. Yet it may also be that in a world where change comes ever more rapidly, we still seek our own lessons from the failure of the Republic and Rome's transformation into Empire.

Chronology

49–45	Civil War
44	Murder of Caesar on the Ides (15th) of March; adoption of Gaius Octavius as Gaius Julius Caesar Octavianus
43	Second Triumvirate of Marcus Antonius, Marcus Aemilius Lepidus and Octavianus; death of Cicero
42	Battle of Philippi; suicide of Marcus Junius Brutus
31	Battle of Actium, Octavianus defeats Antonius and Cleopatra
27	Octavianus receives the title 'Augustus'

Further reading

Primary sources

Livy (59 BC–AD 17) composed his *History of Rome* during the age of the first emperor Augustus. Not all of the 142 books of the *History* have survived, but we do possess Books 1–10 (covering Rome's legendary past and the early years of the Republic) and Books 21–45 (the Second Punic War and Roman expansion down to 167). In his Preface, Livy expressed his pride in 'putting on record the story of the greatest nation in the world'. He attributed Rome's rise to the morality and *pietas* of the early Romans, and mourned the moral decline that he believed led to the Republic's collapse and 'the dark dawning of our modern day when we can neither endure our vices nor face the remedies needed to cure them'. For an introduction, see P. G. Walsh, *Livy: His Historical Aims and Methods*, 2nd edn. (Bristol, 1989), and J. D. Chaplin and C. S. Kraus, *Livy* (Oxford, 2009). On Livy's contemporary Virgil (70–19 BC), whose epic poem the *Aeneid* to a degree expresses similar views, see P. Hardie, *Virgil's Aeneid: Cosmos and Imperium* (Oxford, 1986).

Polybius of Megalopolis (c. 200–c. 118 BC) was one of the Greek hostages taken to Rome in 167 and there wrote the *Histories*. His intention was to explain the dramatic rise of Roman power and to warn his fellow Greeks to avoid provoking Rome's wrath. Polybius' work survives in extensive fragments covering the years 264–146, and in critical skill and proximity to events he is superior to Livy, who used Polybius as a source. See further F. W. Walbank, *Polybius* (Berkeley, 1972).

Under the Roman Empire, the biographer Plutarch (AD c. 46–120) wrote *Parallel Lives* that compared leading figures of ancient

Greece and Rome. Some of the Roman *Lives* are lost, notably that of Scipio Africanus, but the extant works include Coriolanus (used by Shakespeare), Fabius Maximus Cunctator, Cato the Elder, the Gracchi, and the warlords of the 1st century. Plutarch was a biographer rather than an historian and so focused on moral character more than factual detail, but his *Lives* are highly valuable especially for years for which we lack historical narratives. On Plutarch, see C. P. Jones, *Plutarch and Rome* (Oxford, 1971), and T. Duff, *Plutarch's Lives: Exploring Virtue and Vice* (Oxford, 1999).

Cicero (106–43) and Caesar (100–44) both appear below in the chapter bibliographies. For the modern historian the most valuable of Cicero's numerous writings are his letters, on which see G. O. Hutchinson, *Cicero's Correspondence: A Literary Study* (Oxford, 1998). For Caesar's writings, above all his *Commentaries on the Gallic War*, see K. Welch and A. Powell (eds.), *Julius Caesar as Artful Reporter: The War Commentaries as Political Instruments* (London, 1998).

Accessible English translations of all these sources are readily available through the Penguin Classics series and the Loeb Classical Library. Many can also be found online, particularly through LacusCurtius: A Gateway to Ancient Rome (http://penelope. uchicago.edu/Thayer/E/Roman/home.html) and the Perseus Digital Library (www.perseus.tufts.edu).

General works

The bibliography on the Roman Republic is vast. For further reading on all aspects of Republican history, see the articles collected in H. I. Flower (ed.), *The Cambridge Companion to the Roman Republic* (Cambridge, 2004), and N. Rosenstein and R. Morstein-Marx (eds.), *A Companion to the Roman Republic* (Oxford, 2006). Older introductions to the Republic can be found in M. Crawford, *The Roman Republic*, 2nd edn. (London, 1992), and M. Grant, *The World of Rome* (London, 1960), while the story of Rome is continued in C. Kelly, *The Roman Empire: A Very Short Introduction* (Oxford, 2006).

Chapter 1: The mists of the past

On the much debated early history of Rome, see T. J. Cornell, *The Beginnings of Rome: Italy and Rome from the Bronze Age to the Punic Wars (c. 1000–264 BC)* (London, 1995), and G. Forsythe,

A Critical History of Early Rome: From Prehistory to the First Punic War (Berkeley, 2005). On the Roman legendary past, see also M. Fox, *Roman Historical Myths: The Regal Period in Augustan Literature* (Oxford, 1996), and on Rome's Etruscan background, G. Barker and T. Rasmussen, *The Etruscans* (Oxford, 1998).

Chapter 2: The Republic takes shape

In addition to Cornell and Forsythe above, the early expansion of Rome is described in J.-M. David, *The Roman Conquest of Italy* (Oxford, 1996). An introduction to Republican political structures is provided by A. W. Lintott, *The Constitution of the Roman Republic* (Oxford, 1999), while on the Conflict of the Orders, see R. E. Mitchell, *Patricians and Plebeians: The Origin of the Roman State* (Ithaca, 1990), and K. A. Raaflaub (ed.), *Social Struggles in Archaic Rome: New Perspectives on the Conflict of the Orders*, revised edn. (Oxford, 2005).

Chapter 3: Men, women, and the gods

The pressures that the demands of *dignitas* and *gloria* placed on the Roman aristocracy are a central theme of W. V. Harris, *War and Imperialism in Republican Rome 327–70 BC* (Oxford, 1979). See also H. I. Flower, *Ancestor Masks and Aristocratic Power in Roman Culture* (Oxford, 1996), and M. Beard, *The Roman Triumph* (Cambridge, Mass., 2007). Roman society below the elite is explored in J. P. Toner, *Popular Culture in Ancient Rome* (Cambridge, 2009), and R. C. Knapp, *Invisible Romans: Prostitutes, Outlaws, Slaves, Gladiators, Ordinary Men and Women...the Romans that History Forgot* (London, 2011). For more detailed studies of the crucial institution of Roman slavery, see K. R. Bradley, *Slavery and Society at Rome* (Cambridge, 1994), and S. R. Joshel, *Slavery in the Roman World* (Cambridge, 2010).

Roman family life is described in K. R. Bradley, *Discovering the Roman Family: Studies in Roman Social History* (New York and Oxford, 1991), and B. Rawson (ed.), *Marriage, Divorce, and Children in Ancient Rome* (Canberra and Oxford, 1991). On the political and religious status of Roman women, see R. A. Bauman, *Women and Politics in Ancient Rome* (London, 1992), and A. Staples, *From Good Goddess to Vestal Virgins: Sex and Category in Roman Religion* (London, 1998), while one famous Roman matron is brought to life in S. Dixon, *Cornelia: Mother of the Gracchi* (London, 2007).

J. Scheid, *An Introduction to Roman Religion* (Edinburgh, 2003) is a good starting point on the diverse Roman religious world. For more in-depth analysis, see J. Rüpke (ed.), *A Companion to Roman Religion* (Oxford, 2007), and M. Beard, J. North, and S. R. F. Price, *Religions of Rome*, 2 vols (Cambridge, 1998).

Chapter 4: Carthage must be destroyed

R. Miles, *Carthage Must Be Destroyed: The Rise and Fall of an Ancient Civilization* (London, 2010), and S. Lancel, *Carthage: A History* (Oxford, 1995) provide accessible introductions to the Republic's greatest enemy. On the Punic Wars, see A. Goldsworthy, *The Fall of Carthage: The Punic Wars 265–146 BC* (London, 2003), and for an evocative reading of Hannibal's most famous victory, see G. Daly, *Cannae: The Experience of Battle in the Second Punic War* (London, 2002).

Chapter 5: Mistress of the Mediterranean

Rome's encounter with the Greek east is described in detail in E. S. Gruen, *The Hellenistic World and the Coming of Rome*, 2 vols. (Berkeley, 1984). See also A. N. Sherwin-White, *Roman Foreign Policy in the East, 168 BC to AD 1* (London, 1984), and, from a rather different perspective, S. E. Alcock, *Graecia Capta: The Landscapes of Roman Greece* (Cambridge, 1993). A. E. Astin, *Cato the Censor* (Oxford, 1978) presents the career of the great critic of Roman philhellenism, while the documentary evidence for Roman–Greek relations is collected in R. K. Sherk (ed.), *Rome and the Greek East to the Death of Augustus* (Cambridge, 1984).

Chapter 6: The cost of empire

The social and economic crises of the 2nd century are well presented in N. Rosenstein, *Rome at War: Farms, Families, and Death in the Middle Republic* (Chapel Hill, 2004). D. Stockton, *The Gracchi* (Oxford, 1979) remains an excellent introduction, while on Marius and Sulla, see R. J. Evans, *Gaius Marius: A Political Biography* (Pretoria, 1994), and A. Keaveney, *Sulla: The Last Republican*, 2nd edn. (London, 2005). On the military developments that played such a crucial role in the Republic's collapse, see also L. De Blois, *The Roman Army and Politics in the First Century BC* (Amsterdam, 1987), and A. Keaveney, *The Army in the Roman Revolution* (London, 2007).

Chapter 7: Word and image

For an overview of Roman literary culture, see S. J. Harrison (ed.), *The Blackwell Companion to Latin Literature* (Oxford, 2005). On the early comic playwrights, see D. Konstan, *Roman Comedy* (Ithaca, 1983), and T. J. Moore, *Plautus and His Audience* (Austin, 2000), and on the 1st century T. P. Wiseman, *Catullus and His World* (Cambridge, 1985). A sympathetic introduction to Cicero's life and writings is given by E. Rawson, *Cicero: A Portrait*, revised edn. (Bristol, 1983), and his political career is set in context in T. Wiedemann, *Cicero and the End of the Roman Republic* (London, 1994).

Accessible surveys of Republican art and architecture are provided by N. H. Ramage and A. Ramage, *Roman Art: Romulus to Constantine*, 5th edn. (Upper Saddle River, 2009), and M. Beard and J. Henderson, *Classical Art: From Greece to Rome* (Oxford, 2001). On the archaeology of Rome itself, see A. Claridge, *Rome: An Archaeological Guide* (Oxford, 1998), and on the transformation of Roman material culture under Augustus, see still P. Zanker, *The Power of Images in the Age of Augustus* (Michigan, 1988).

Chapter 8: The last years

Overviews of the dramatic events of the Republic's final years are provided by D. Shotter, *The Fall of the Roman Republic*, 2nd edn. (London, 2005), and M. Beard and M. Crawford, *Rome in the Late Republic: Problems and Interpretations*, 2nd edn. (London, 1999), and from a more popular perspective, by T. Holland, *Rubicon: The Triumph and Tragedy of the Roman Republic* (London, 2004).

For biographies of the last generation of Roman warlords, see among many others P. Southern, *Pompey the Great* (Stroud, 2002), and R. Seager, *Pompey: A Political Biography*, 2nd edn. (Oxford, 2002); B. A. Marshall, *Crassus: A Political Biography* (Amsterdam, 1976); C. Meier, *Caesar* (London, 1995), and A. Goldsworthy, *Caesar: The Life of a Colossus* (London, 2007).

On the transition from Republic to Empire, one should still read R. Syme, *The Roman Revolution* (Oxford, 1939), and also K. Raaflaub and M. Toher (eds.), *Between Republic and Empire: Interpretations of Augustus and His Principate* (Berkeley, 1990).

Finally, the period between Gaius Marius and Augustus is brought to life in great detail in the *Masters of Rome* series of novels by Colleen McCullough.

Chapter 9: The afterlife of the Republic

Very Short Introductions already exist for the Roman Empire, Augustine, Machiavelli, Shakespeare, Rousseau, and the French Revolution.

For an overview of the Republic's enduring influence as a political ideal, see F. Millar, *The Roman Republic in Political Thought* (Hanover, 2002).

On Augustine's vision of history, see R. A. Markus, *Saeculum: History and Society in the Theology of St Augustine*, revised edn. (Cambridge, 1988), while for an introduction to his greatest work, read G. O'Daly, *Augustine's City of God: A Reader's Guide* (Oxford, 1999).

Machiavelli's vision of Rome and Republicanism is explored in J. A. Pocock, *The Machiavellian Moment: Florentine Political Thought and the Atlantic Republican Tradition* (Princeton, 1975), and V. Sullivan, *Machiavelli's Three Romes: Religion, Human Liberty, and Politics Reformed* (DeKalb, 1996). There are a number of recent studies of Shakespeare's relationship to ancient Rome, which include W. Chernaik, *The Myth of Rome in Shakespeare and His Contemporaries* (Cambridge, 2011), and G. Wills, *Rome and Rhetoric: Shakespeare's Julius Caesar* (New Haven, 2011).

The significance of the Roman Republic in the creation of the United States of America is discussed in C. J. Richard, *The Founders and the Classics: Greece, Rome, and the American Enlightenment* (Cambridge, 1994), and M. N. S. Sellers, *American Republicanism: Roman Ideology in the United States Constitution* (New York, 1994). For Rome and the French Revolution, see R. L. Herbert, *David, Voltaire, 'Brutus' and the French Revolution: An Essay in Art and Politics* (London, 1972), and L. Althusser, *Politics and History: Montesquieu, Rousseau, Hegel and Marx*, 2nd edn. (London, 1977). For an overview of Rome's influence on the 17th and 18th centuries, see now E. G. Andrew, *Imperial Republics: Revolution, War and Territorial Expansion from the English Civil War to the French Revolution* (Toronto, 2011).

Perceptions of ancient Rome in more modern times can be traced through C. Edwards (ed.), *Roman Presences: Receptions of Rome in European Culture, 1789–1945* (Cambridge, 1999), P. Bondanella, *The Eternal City: Roman Images in the Modern World* (North Carolina, 1987), and M. Wyke, *Projecting the Past: Ancient Rome, Cinema and History* (London, 1997).

Index

Index

Expand your collection of
VERY SHORT INTRODUCTIONS

HISTORY
A Very Short Introduction
John H. Arnold

History: A Very Short Introduction is a stimulating essay about how we understand the past. The book explores various questions provoked by our understanding of history, and examines how these questions have been answered in the past. Using examples of how historians work, the book shares the sense of excitement at discovering not only the past, but also ourselves.

'A stimulating and provocative introduction to one of collective humanity's most important quests – understanding the past and its relation to the present. A vivid mix of telling examples and clear cut analysis.'

David Lowenthal, University College London

'This is an extremely engaging book, lively, enthusiastic and highly readable, which presents some of the fundamental problems of historical writing in a lucid and accessible manner. As an invitation to the study of history it should be difficult to resist.'

Peter Burke, Emmanuel College, Cambridge

www.oup.com/vsi/

ROMAN BRITAIN
A Very Short Introduction
Peter Salway

Britain was within the orbit of Graeco-Roman civilization for at least half a millenium, and for over 350 years part of the political union created by the Roman Empire that encompassed most of Europe and all the countries of the Mediterranean.

First published as part of the best-selling *Oxford Illustrated History of Britain*, Peter Salway's Very Short Introduction to Roman Britain weaves together the results of archaeological investigation and historical scholarship in a rounded and highly readable concise account. He charts the history of Britain from the first invasion under Julius Casear ro the final collapse of the Romano-British way of life in the 5th century AD.

www.oup.com/vsi/